The Silicon Idol

The Silicon Idol

The micro revolution and its social implications

MICHAEL SHALLIS

SCHOCKEN BOOKS · NEW YORK

First American edition published by Schocken Books 1984

10 9 8 7 6 5 4 3 2 1   84 85 86 87

Copyright © 1984 by Michael Shallis

Published by agreement with Oxford University Press, Oxford

Library of Congress Cataloging in Publication Data
Shallis, Michael.
The Silicon Idol.
Bibliography: p.
Includes Index.
1. Computers   2. Computers—Social aspects.
I. Title
QA76.S47   1984   303.4'834   84 – 5296

Set by Cotswold Typesetting Ltd, Gloucester
Printed in Great Britain by
Billings & Sons Ltd, Worcester

0-8052-3927-8

PREFACE

It seems that any critic of technology is liable to be labelled a Luddite and I would not be surprised if the term was used about myself by some of the readers of this book. The term Luddite implies someone who is anti-progressive, who wants to go back to the past. It derives from the probably imaginary character Ned Ludd, who reputedly encouraged the stocking weavers of the English Midlands in the early nineteenth century to smash the weaving frames that were depriving traditional craftsmen of a livelihood.

There are two points I would like to make about the Luddites. One is that these were people taking action to save their jobs and means of living in the face of a socially disruptive and imposed technology: an expression of political commitment and personal anger which seems to me to be worthy at least of respect. The second point is about progress. I do not think new technology for technology's sake, or even for the sake of efficiency and productivity, is *progressive* if the price paid for such progress is unemployment, urbanization or the removal of skill, pride and tradition from the dispossessed people involved. Progress should be aimed at some specified goal and can only be judged in terms of that goal. Progress should not automatically imply new in place of the old, if the old is actually satisfactory. Nor does criticizing the new automatically mean that the critic wants to return to the past. Rather it means that the new does not live up to the existing expectations and that new things need to be better than the old before they should replace what is good from the past. Of course, no one need defend what is bad from the past and I certainly do not intend to do that. Criticism of the new may simply imply a notion of conservation.

I would accept the term Luddite about myself if it implied that I do not think ends necessarily justify means. If Luddite means the preservation of all that is good from the past and the rejection of things that destroy that good, then I would welcome

the term. What I do not welcome is the fact that supporters of the new technology have often used that term to silence their critics and make discussion one-sided. The distinct lack of much criticism of computers in public is in remarkable contrast to the fears and misgivings heard in private about a technology advanced, and advanced rapidly, by technocrats and governments and inserted into the fabric of our society before most people even get a chance to understand what it is all about. With this book I attempt to redress that imbalance.

My own involvement with computers is surprisingly long. My interest in the new technology in the latter half of the 1960s prompted me to return to university as a mature student at the age of 27. Over the last thirteen years I have worked with large main-frame computers and single chip micros. I have programmed in several languages and been intimately connected with both scientific number-crunching and integrating a mini-computer into a sophisticated experimental apparatus. More recently I have taught students in various groups about computers and programming, and also about the ideas contained in this book. Like many people involved in computers and new technology my academic discipline is not in computing science, but in astrophysics. My expertise has, however, allowed me to understand, use, and advise people about computing technology in educational, commercial and scientific circles. But I have never owned a computer and, with the exception of once owning a digital watch for two years, never will.

What I have attempted in this book is to present, in as many different ways as possible, views of what computers are. The first half deals with computers, their workings, applications and projected futures. The second half is concerned with their historical and social origins and the effects that they are having on employment and the structure of our society. The book ends with an assessment of the ideas that lie behind the advances in the machines, and of where that leaves people. If my conclusions seem pessimistic then that is unintentional; I do have faith in common sense and in the ability of people to discriminate and to recognize things for what they are. That faith has been borne out in my contact with a wide range of people to whom I have presented, and with whom I have discussed, the material that makes up this book. The refinement of many of my ideas, and hence the improvement of this book, is also due partly to those people—students, colleagues and friends. I acknowledge their important and stimulating role with thanks.

I have also received more specific advice and critical comment from several people: Frank Pettit, John Parker, Marie and Dennis O'Malley, and Max Gorman on specific points; and Robert Elmore, Alan Ryan, Simon Pringle, Richard Conrad, OP, Ann Buckle and Jonathan Darby on the whole manuscript. Their patience, constructive criticism, encouragement and support have been very much appreciated and I thank them whole-heartedly. David Black inspired many of my own thoughts and his comments on the manuscript were invaluable. To him I offer heartfelt thanks. I am also very grateful to Leslie Watts and Susan Hugo-Hamman for typing the manuscript. To my wife, Esther, and my family I extend my appreciation for their love and understanding during the months of writing. Without them this work would not have been possible.

Lastly I owe thanks to Dr Henry Hardy for his faith in the book from the time of its commissioning through to its final form. His editorial hand has helped me considerably and enabled my hopes to be realized within these covers.

Oxford   M. J. S.
1983

CONTENTS

LIST OF FIGURES

Lastly, I would address one general admonition to all; that they consider what are the true ends of knowledge, and that they seek it not either for pleasure of mind, or for contention, or for superiority to others, or for profit, or fame, or power, or any of these inferior things; but for the benefit and use of life; and that they perfect and govern it in charity. For it was from lust of power that the angels fell, from lust of knowledge that men fell, but of charity there can be no excess, neither did angel or man ever come in danger by it.

Francis Bacon, *The Great Instauration*

1 MACHINES THAT 'THINK'

There are two responses to the problem of what mankind should do if alien intelligences, little green men or what-have-you, are discovered elsewhere in the universe. The first attitude is one of optimism, joy at knowing that we are not alone in the universe and that such beings should be contacted as rapidly as possible. They may, after all, be able to help us with all our terrestrial problems, improve our economies, rid us of our weapons and show us how to live happily. The other attitude is quite the opposite and presupposes that the aliens are just as likely to be hostile as peaceable and we had better keep ourselves quiet, unnoticed, to avoid being desolated by these potential space invaders.

These two characteristic extremes of opinion are also to be found in people's reaction to modern computing technology. The optimists are rapturous towards new techniques and technologies, overlook the dangers of 'invasion' and regard the technology as being nothing short of an all-purpose saviour. Others view new technology with suspicion and even fear. Such feelings may arise from the possibility of losing one's job, of being replaced by a machine, or they may stem from some irrational foreboding about computers, seen as machines that 'think'.

Although these are extreme points in a spectrum of opinion about computer technology the interesting thing is how similar the attitude to computers is in comparison with that towards extra-terrestrial intelligence. Somehow computers appear like aliens from another planet; somehow they seem to be more than just mere machines. It is as if we have been invaded, so that we now find around us 'intelligent' washing machines, cars that 'think', and computers standing in for doctors, engineers, designers and other experts. People want to know what the computer has to tell us, as if the computer was a form of 'little green man'. Above all other technologies it is computer technology that has rapidly become highly anthropomorphized.

I do not want to push the analogy with extra-terrestrial intelligence too far, although the thought that microtechnology is somehow 'alien' has its appeal. The point to be made is simply that people do project an almost lifelike quality into machines that makes them look as if they 'think'. Because people, in order to operate a computer, have to put information and instructions into the machine and receive information back out of it, they equate such a process with communication, which is something people normally do with other people. Hence a jargon builds up and phrases like 'talking to a computer', 'communications interfacing', 'machines talking to each other' and so on, creep into daily language. These phrases reinforce the anthropomorphic image we have of computers and so the tendency to discuss these machines as 'intelligent', 'creative', and 'thinking', soon becomes commonplace. Such language is nothing other than jargon, but it is deceptive jargon, because its use undermines the language used and alters our very perception of the machines and our attitudes towards them. It is only when we are capable of projecting an image of a wise man on to some black boxes, a keyboard and a television screen that we become confident in 'telling' the machine our inmost thoughts (if the computer is acting as if it were a psychiatrist) or our most intimate and embarrassing medical symptoms (if the machine is programmed to perform medical diagnosis). The irony is that, when some people do respond to a machine in this way, they actually prefer it to a real doctor, can talk more truthfully and feel a greater sense of confidentiality towards it than to another human being. This happens partly because it is an 'impersonal' machine and partly because the machine is somehow like an ideal person, an alien intelligence maybe.

Machines that 'talk back' hold a fascination, almost hypnotic, that many people just cannot resist. The anthropomorphized machine really can evoke an emotional response from people that is hard to distinguish from genuine human feelings—until you stop to think about it. By questioning the act of 'communication' with the computer it is possible to see more objectively just what one's involvement with it is turning into. However, even when people have written their own computer program and so are fully aware that the machine is only following instructions they have devised, it can still bewitch them into half believing that the machine is somehow a 'person'. It is the same fascination as the talking doll, the ventriloquist's dummy and the mechanical singing bird and it is a powerful fascination.

Added to that spellbinding power is the computer's inbuilt complexity, its inner sets of rules, which, acting like a puzzle, provoke some people into a compulsive desire to 'break the code'. Such people are called *hackers* and they are to be found in most computer installations, living almost literally for and through the machine.

The hacker spends his life in the artificial environment of the computer terminal room, eating junk food while he pours over computer print-out and constantly returns to his console to try to manipulate the system again. Although the lifestyle of the hacker seems unfamiliar there is something of his psychology in most of us. The hypnotic effect of the TV monitor draws people into the life of the machine. Computer games become compulsive, the interactive program (the sort that 'talks' back to you, often by name) invokes our attention in the way that becomes extreme in the hacker. Computer makers and program designers often play on this quality. I remember one computer game that began with the message: 'The purpose of this game is to discover its rules'. You then had to find out appropriate ways of responding, urged on by messages that told you whether your response was legitimate or not and which usually deducted points from your given score. Apart from the frustration it invoked, it also had its fascination. One wanted to win, to beat the system. But this response is not confined to games alone. Obtaining data, which may itself be of no special interest, from a machine is compulsive. When I was running a laboratory experiment some years ago, visitors used to accumulate around the bench because the results of the experiment were continuously being written up, by the computer controlling the apparatus, on to a television monitor. Whenever someone passed by they would stand and watch, hypnotized by the computer's output. It was engrossing even if rather meaningless. This quality of the computer to draw people towards it, to bind their attention, can be played upon in teaching people to use computers. An interactive program that conducts a 'dialogue' with students 'helps' them through the learning task and students seem to enjoy being led through an exercise by a machine that appears to be so patient and concerned.

I have used the comparison between computers and alien creatures but an alternative analogy could be drawn between these machines and a domestic animal. The machine, like a dog, seems to be under your control and yet able to respond to you of its own free will. I said we project the image of a wise man on to computers, and this is not unlike the way we project some of our needs on to pets. It is no coincidence that one of the more popular home computers is called a PET, because this quality of computers to respond to our projections is understood, at least in so far as the marketing of machines goes. However, that quality is more than an advertising gimmick, it is a part of our anthropomorphic attitude to computers, an attitude encouraged by the computer industry and encouraged in order to reduce our resistance to the machines. That resistance stems not from the euphoric response to computers but from the opposite attitude to them, namely fear.

I know many people who have a deep-seated suspicion of much technology but especially of computers. The fear is usually only partly conscious and often unexpressed until released in conversation, but it is nevertheless there. There is something about this technology that people do not like. Part of it may be because the machine does take over, does pull you into its world. It can create obsession, as all computer programmers (and their wives) will tell you. It also intervenes between people, replacing human relationships with machine interaction, and it intervenes between man and nature in ways that are deceptively 'useful' but that can be recognized as an artificial substitute for experience and unnatural. The fear may stem, at least in part, from knowing that the hardest thing with computers is to switch them off. It also stems from the same thing that makes computers compulsive, their ability to receive our projections, our making them 'lifelike'. To imagine that a machine is in some way like a person is not just to say something about the machine but rather to reveal an attitude to people. The anthropomorphized machine is a reflection of a mechanized view of man. This is where dislike of computers also comes from.

We do not like what we ourselves have become and which is reflected in our technology.

It may seem that some of the attitudes I have been describing are extreme and that surely the computer is nothing more than a tool, just as a motor car is or a garden spade. We do not, in general, have strong feelings about garden spades, even if we may become more emotional about motor cars. What I am presenting here, however, should be common experience to people involved, however loosely, with computer technology. The machine that 'thinks' does invoke a powerful response, and one that many people find alluring. Professor Joseph Weizenbaum describes in his book *Computer Power and Human Reason* how his attitude to computers was transformed when he saw how people reacted to a program that he had devised as an exercise in language manipulation by a machine. His program could 'respond' like a Rogerian psychotherapist and both psychologists and lay people alike somehow 'believed' the machine was responding to them like a person would. It seemed to 'listen' and it seemed to 'care'.

Weizenbaum stood aside and looked carefully at the pheno-menon that he and his colleagues had created and his book is an invaluable source both of argument and of evidence of human feeling about that aspect of computing called 'artificial intelli-gence'. Weizenbaum's shock at the way people projected their needs on to a computer program was the starting point for his analysis and provides an illustration of the way attitudes to computers are more extreme than towards garden spades. Another example can be found in the hope that the computer will be the solution to our social, economic, even personal problems. We hope, indeed expect, that the techniques of computing will at least help us towards solving the world's problems, as if we only need to find the appropriate technique. Rather than analyse them as 'our problems', which stem from us by definition, we seek to find external solutions and hope that 'something out there' will be the answer we are looking for. The tendency is, however, to regard all problems as nothing more than mismanagement, lack of sufficient resources and so on and to assume that there is automatically a technological solution to the difficulties. In that context the computer appears in the form of a *deus ex machina* that can relieve us from drudgery, raise our standard of living, create wealth, leisure and, presumably, happiness. We, like the hacker, are seduced by technique, into an illusory world.

When people sit down at the computer terminal, whether to play a game, write a piece of program or to run an existing one, their attention gets focused on the technical details of the operations they are involved in. This effect is possibly most apparent when people are new to computers; you can see the technicality of the machine taking over. The trouble with this is twofold. First the intervention of technique isolates people from direct experience, by substituting for the real world the fantasy world of the terminal and television screen. Such isolating and second-hand experience is not wholesome, for it only operates on limited regions of human consciousness. Secondly, technique should be a means of providing a way to achieve some goal, but technique as an end in itself is no end at all. The computer is seen as a continuing part of mankind's progress, but progress implies moving towards an end. The notion of progress, as used in common speech, never signifies that end, and the idea of progress itself becomes an endless concept. When technology is progressive, its development is endless and with no end the technique becomes everything.

The reason why the computer can be almost reasonably regarded as a general solution to our problems is that it is designed to be a general-purpose machine. It is a machine that 'thinks' and can therefore be set to 'thinking' about any desired subject matter. It can be argued that in order to get it to 'think' the subject matter has to be analysed in such a careful and objective way that the problem will become clear and the outcome of the 'thinking', therefore, will be 'correct'. In computing circles there is a well-known phrase—garbage in, garbage out—which corrects any impression people may have that what the computer says is right; it is only as good as what is put into it. Nevertheless we project an attitude on to the machine which then reflects an aspect of ourselves. Maybe by allowing the computer to solve our problems for us we, in some way, absolve ourselves of our incapacity to take responsibility for our lives, to sort out our own mess. How comforting to allow the machine to take over so that we can then enjoy ourselves.

'For the first time on earth' reads the headline of one

computer advertisement, showing a small computer against a back-drop of stars, implying the descent from the skies of a problem solver. Another claims that 'within a day you will be talking to it like a new friend', where 'it' is a small computer. The claim is untrue, but the anthropomorphic attitude is quite clear. In much promotional material the implication, there in one guise or another, is that computers are almost human because they are machines that 'think'.

It will be noticed that many words in this text, words like 'think', 'intelligence', etc., have been placed in quotation marks; this has been done partly to emphasize the anthropomorphic language used about computers and partly to make the following point. Because the computer appears to 'think' and because in order to make use of it the operator needs to 'communicate' with it, in the sense of passing information into the machine and receiving results from it, the computer has rapidly become personalized; it virtually 'presents itself' as an android. Computing technology has enabled man–machine 'communication' to become increasingly 'human'. There are now computers that can recognize the human voice, in a limited context, and many machines that literally 'talk' back to you. For example, there are children's educational toys that 'talk' to the child through spelling and arithmetic instruction. There is now available a computerized coffee machine that 'speaks' and a car that 'talks' to its driver. I will deal later with the technicalities of such things, for now it is enough to note that the technology itself is developing along the path where human faculties are being mimicked in electronic terms and machines are being endorsed with such faculties. Increasingly, computers are being extended by being provided with the equivalent of human senses; they are being built to give the appearance that they can 'read', 'talk', 'write', 'touch', 'see' and 'walk about'. Even more, at the research frontiers, machines are being designed to 'learn'.

The question arises whether machines can 'talk' or 'think'. I use the words in quotation marks simply to draw out this question. Such words are used, of course, largely to 'humanize' the machines, to make them more acceptable to people, but in this way machines are being endowed with qualities they do not in fact possess. Computer people end by believing what their own words have led them to believe and in the process have undermined the language we apply, correctly, to ourselves. To say that a machine 'thinks' is to use the word 'think' as jargon. Jargon is defined not only as technical language but also as debased or illiterate speech. To talk of computers 'thinking' is not the usual form of English but jargon in both its senses. To ascribe human faculties to computers is to debase the language and demean human characteristics, as well as to project inappropriate qualities on to the machines. The jargon also works in reverse, with people being described as 'information processing animals' who can be 'programmed'.

The use of quotation marks is important, to distinguish between the genuine use of language and the application of it to processes that may simulate aspects of human functions but which are nevertheless not human processes. In the literature, words like 'knowledge' were always found in quotation marks and Weizenbaum, in *Computer Power and Human Reason*, quotes an anonymous author writing presumably in the early 1970s and saying: 'Only a year or two ago, it was necessary to put quotation marks around the word "knowledge" whenever it was used in such a context as this . . . but there is a consensus that we have reached the threshold beyond which one can think of computers as having knowledge' (p. 244).

The quotation marks are being dropped, which signifies a change from projecting human qualities on to computers to actually believing the machines now possess those qualities. However, when we think about *thinking*, we realize that thinking is more than just passing information through a 'computer' (the brain) but involves the whole person. Computers, at best, might simulate part or even all of the brain, but they do not possess the qualities that go to make up a whole person. To attribute such qualities to them may help people to relate to computers, may make the machines more *user friendly* (to use the jargon), but it also fuels those irrational fears.

In order to distinguish man from machine I present an outline here of what I mean by human qualities, in order to have a basis or standard against which comparisons can be made elsewhere in the book. The account I give of man's qualities and ideals is based partly on E. F. Schumacher's incomparable book *A Guide for the Perplexed* and stems from a traditional and religious attitude to the world. There are other views, of course, and there is much discussion and speculation about human nature in modern thought, but it seems to me that what little consensus there is nowadays scarcely matches up to mankind's traditional view of the human condition, which stands in stark contrast to the description of man as an animated computer.

Man is a hierarchical being in a hierarchical world. The common feature of our material world is *matter* itself, substance; and matter forms the lowest level of the hierarchy of man's being. The second ingredient of the human condition is *life*, which we recognize when we see it, even if we cannot define it accurately. A dead dog is qualitatively different from a live dog. People share the quality of life with the plant and animal kingdoms. Next we add to the human structure the property of *consciousness*, the ability to discern, to reason, to evaluate, to choose. Consciousness is more than just being able to think; it enables a creature to be in the world. It is less clear where the dividing line comes between which animals are and which are not conscious, but clearly the higher animals share this quality with mankind. Finally human beings possess the quality of *self-transcendence*, the gift that enables man to strive upwards; the quality that helps us to discern right from wrong, to recognize the Absolute. This quality seems to belong to mankind alone of all creatures. Above this level are higher realms unattainable to us, although our self-transcendent selves can be aware of their existence. There are also realms below that of matter, but the four levels I have described add up to the whole person.

The extraordinary thing is that life, consciousness and self-transcendence are all quite mysterious. We do not understand them at all. Neither do we understand matter. We are made of mysteries. Yet, despite that, we can discern these qualities. A dead computer (one that is switched off) appears indistinguishable from a live one. The machine is just matter. We need a pilot light to indicate to us that the machine is turned on. With living creatures we can see life, even though scientists cannot track it down. Self-transcendence is much harder to perceive and is consequently not always recognized as distinct from consciousness, but there are enough examples around us of people who do strive for good, for light, for love, to enable us to discern this more ephemeral quality.

The trouble with computers comes in our discernment of

consciousness. To see our ability to think as being the property of an active brain—that is reducing consciousness to an interaction of life and matter—is to misplace the quality, to ignore that it has its own level. That is only a step away from regarding thought as a 'mechanical' process and towards making the inevitable comparison between the computer's electronic circuitry and the human brain. We don't believe computers are alive, but we mistake their operation for a form of consciousness, because consciousness itself has been incorrectly understood. In addition, this confusion is augmented by the ability of the human nervous system to affect and be affected by the electrical operation of the computer circuits. There are many cases known of people's psychological state adversely affecting the performance of a computer system and likewise of people becoming ill, dizzy or even mildly epileptic in the presence of computing machinery. There are computer disrupters and computer 'healers', people with an ability to get malfunctioning machines working again without doing much more than being present. It seems to me that there is some interaction between consciousness and electricity that makes the machine that 'thinks' appear to be conscious, because we sense something about it that distinguishes it from a purely mechanical piece of apparatus.

Traditional wisdom also distinguishes between the rational mind—*ratio*—and the intellect—*intellectus*. The rational mind is associated with consciousness and the brain, whilst the intellect corresponds to self-transcendence and is symbolically located in the heart. Hence the mind rules the emotions through the heart, the organ by which we perceive wisdom and which makes us truly human. Intelligence, then, traditionally implies a person's means of access to that which is central and essential to the human condition and which becomes manifest through acts of charity, good works and love. To reduce intelligence to mere reason is like reducing self-transcendence to consciousness and thereby reducing the human condition to a level below its potential, which is therefore degrading and unwholesome.

In this context the notion of 'machine intelligence' is nonsensical and can only be rephrased as 'machine simulation of rationality' or some such description. Nevertheless I will be referring to artificial and machine 'intelligence' in this book because it is an area of great importance in the discussion of computers. Clearly though, in a hierarchical world-picture, machines cannot be 'intelligent', if by intelligence we mean the highest function of the human condition, linking mankind with the Absolute. It is clear, in the computer context, that we are talking about a reduced concept of intelligence that means *the ability to appear conscious through rational or logical information processing*. That definition conveys what I mean when I use the phrase 'artificial (or machine) intelligence'.

The fact that the word 'intelligence' is used in discussing computers is another aspect of the way people display their anthropomorphic view of the machine and my comments about language and anthropomorphism contain elements that are central issues in this book. The language is no longer confined to the research laboratories but spills over into mundane usage, such as referring to the 'intelligent washing machine'. In computer circles 'artificial intelligence' is defined as that characteristic displayed by a machine, which in a human would be judged as intelligence. It is a description that relates to appearances. If it is argued that machines are not intelligent, that is they do not think, then the response may well be thus: does a person display intelligence when he performs some such operation as doing arithmetic or reading a thermometer? If the answer to this question is yes then it follows that computers also display intelligence because they can do arithmetic or read a thermometer. These are simple examples, of course, and later in this book far more complex computer applications will be dealt with, but their simplicity illustrates starkly the force of this approach.

There are four points I want to make about this argument for 'machine intelligence', the first of which is concerned purely with the notion of *intelligence* and its confusion with the idea of *thinking*. Thinking is not necessarily the same as rationality or consciousness, but is a much more general expression of 'mental processes'. I do not want to argue that machines cannot 'think', in the sense that they simulate what in humans would be termed thinking, neither would I want to argue that machines could not 'think better' than human beings can, for clearly in terms of speed and accuracy, for example, they can perform calculations much better than people do. My point is that 'thinking' is not the same as intelligence, which I have described above, and intelligence is a higher attribute, concerned with wisdom. Machines may be clever, but they are not wise.

The second point to make about arguments for 'machine intelligence' is that they are invariably rooted in a particular view of man; that he is nothing but a biological, self-preserving, information-processing creature. The view is already anthropomorphic towards the machines and man becomes redefined as their reflection. Human qualities and perceptions, the essence that distinguishes life from the non-living, have been squeezed out of the view of man in such a reductionist picture. The man–machine comparison excludes man's personal consciousness, does not regard the mind as something greater than the brain and denies any spiritual dimensions to reality. The notion of 'machine intelligence' is firmly rooted in that ideology.

The next point to make concerns a certain circularity of argument. Any objection of the form that makes a distinction between a human response to a situation and that of a machine can be countered by imagining a more powerful machine that has been designed to answer the criticism. Any criticism then offered can be defended by yet another imagined machine. I shall return to this argument shortly and mention my final point which is simply the question of purpose.

To take the example above, the difference between a person reading a thermometer and a computer doing the same task can be viewed in terms of purpose. The person is curious about the temperature and reads the thermometer to find it out. A computer, linked to a thermometer, can relay the information it obtains from the temperature gauge to the outside world, maybe via a television screen, or it may use the value obtained as some intermediate step in a process that will result in an external display. Its purpose can only be that of its user, even if its user is impersonal, such as a relay switch on a thermostat. Computers do not just 'sit and think' for the pleasure of it, neither do they read temperatures out of curiosity and to argue that you could design one to do that is sheer anthropomorphism gone mad.

Alan Turing, who is regarded as one of the founders of computer science in the 1940s, took an operational attitude to such questions as intelligence and thinking, that is he regarded the test for intelligence as a practical matter entirely, one that could be defined by performing an operation. If doing arithmetic was the operation that suitably defined intelligence then a machine would be intelligent if it could perform that operation. He devised what is now referred to as the Turing Test for thinking machines, which is based on this notion. A person is placed in a room with two computer terminals; one of them is connected to a computer and the other is linked to another human being. Using the two terminals to communicate, the person testing the system has to try to guess which terminal is connected to a computer, which to a person. A computer can be said to pass this test and to 'think' if it cannot be distinguished from the human being, whom we credit with being able to think.

The trouble with such a test is twofold. Firstly it depends on reducing 'thinking' to something so stripped of human connotations and qualities, that it could be argued that it no longer resembles thinking. For example, personal consciousness, experience and awareness must not be tested for, although these are essential elements of human thought. The other snag is the question of circularity of argument already mentioned: you can always imagine a machine that could answer any question, counter any probe that the tester could devise, so 'proving' the case for machine-thought by brute force.

The real trouble with the Turing test however lies in the fact that terminals have to be used instead of direct confrontation. Thought and response to questions are patently something more than providing words on television screens. The test does not allow for this; it denies human qualities and equates, quite inappropriately, machine performance with human interaction. Such an equation only impoverishes people's view of themselves which can only add to their problems, not help them to solve them. It is a gross case of reflected anthropomorphism and coming from one of the founders of computer science may demonstrate why the attitudes I describe are so prevalent.

In Chapter Seven, I shall deal with the origin of computers, and examine why they were developed and how they came to be developed as they were. Since we are discussing the anthropomorphic attitude towards computers, however, it is worth mentioning here that one suggestion is that computers were built, from their conception, as machines that 'think'; that is, the whole idea behind computers is anthropomorphic. From the earliest days of computer science the notion, indeed the aim, was to build machines that could be intellectually more advanced than man, the notion of the Ultra-Intelligent Machine. That aim lies behind even the most trivial micro-technology application. The notion, I suggest, is based on a mistake, because it assumes that intelligence is an abstract, and operationally definable, quality. It is also mistaken because it springs from an impoverished view of man. That is not to say that machines that can outstrip man's performance in some mental tasks cannot be built, for plainly they have been, but that the implications that lie behind the idea of Ultra-Intelligence are false. It is akin to the notion of welcoming alien space invaders as saviours of mankind; it is also akin to Frankenstein's desire to play God and produce a creature with the qualities of life, consciousness and self-transcendence. Machines, like Frankenstein's monster, are not human and we cannot put human qualities into them, however much we make the machines simulate some of those qualities. To treat them as being human, even in part, is to be more than short-sighted.

It is our attitude towards technology that seems to me to be so important and especially so with computing technology, if for no other reason than that this new technology has spread so rapidly and has developed so quickly that we can scarcely keep up with the changes it promotes. There is much euphoria about microtechnology but there is also mistrust and fear. In the following chapters I present what I trust is a helpful analysis of the roots of computer technology, where it springs from, as well as an insight into its effect on us all and the implications of its widening horizon of applications. I shall continue to use quotation marks around words that I think are misused to distinguish them as jargon and also to act as a reminder that their use springs from an attitude towards computing technology.

The anthropomorphic attitude, which endows the machine with 'personality', leads along the path that began with Turing and his colleagues and continues towards the goal of 'ultra-intelligence'. That attitude, like the one that seeks for gods to descend from the stars in their flying saucers, places the artifact above man and in place of God. The psalmist recognized this attitude when he wrote of the heathen:

> Their idols are silver and gold,
> The work of men's hands.
> They have mouths, but they speak not;
> Eyes have they, but they see not;
> They have ears, but they hear not;
> Noses have they, but they smell not;
> They have hands, but they handle not;
> Feet have they, but they walk not;
> Neither speak they through their throat.
> They that make them are like unto them;
> So is every one that trusteth in them.

(From Psalm 115 (AV))

From reading the literature, from surveying the presentation of computing technology in the information media, from talking with people about computers, I believe that the euphoric response, the anthropomorphic attitude to computing technology, prevails. The computer, the machine that 'thinks', is rapidly becoming a Silicon Idol.

2 HARDWARE AND SOFTWARE

Computers are not calculating machines, although most computers can calculate. Neither are they information-processing machines, although most computers do process information. The difficulty with many definitions of what computers are is in their specificity. Despite the fact that many computers are designed to perform sometimes even quite specific tasks, those tasks are not a necessary part of defining what computers are. A satisfactory definition is this: *A computer is a machine that obeys an ordered sequence of instructions and can modify those instructions in the light of some intermediate result.* This statement avoids the pitfalls of saying what tasks computers can perform which, in general, will always be in the form of an incomplete list; rather, it defines the machine in terms of the concept of its operation: the computer simply obeys instructions. What those instructions are or how they are obeyed is not relevant to the essence of computers. Above all other considerations, computers are general-purpose or universal machines. They are not designed to do anything in particular, but are built to do anything that can be reduced to the form of a suitable set of instructions.

This definition also draws attention to the two aspects of a computer that are necessary for its operation and they are the concern of this chapter. A computer is a machine; it is made up from physical components that are collectively called hardware. It is, moreover, a machine that obeys instructions which collectively are called software, because they exist in a rather more ephemeral form. The analogy between a computer and a book could be drawn, where the physical book, its pages, the printing ink and so on are the hardware and the content of the words and pictures are the software. A computer needs both these complementary elements, just as a book does.

The obeying of instructions, the hardware interacting with the software, will be described later. The scope for writing instructions is virtually unlimited and the range of ways in which machines obey instructions will be demonstrated in the following chapters. Computers nowadays do not necessarily look like computers. An automated machine tool, a coffee machine, a child's toy, can all be computers, because they can all be machines that obey an ordered sequence of instructions.

However, there is a second part to the definition given above that concerns the modification of the instructions, by the machine, in the light of some intermediate result. The simplest form to satisfy this part of the definition would be one where the sequence in which instructions were obeyed was modified by an intermediate result. For example if a coffee machine is 'computerized', then the sequence of instructions it obeys will be modified depending on whether the user pushes the button for coffee with milk or the one for black coffee. In the two cases a different sequence of obeyed instructions must take place to enable different results to emerge in the form of coffee with or without milk.

The definition is not so specific as that, however, but merely states that instructions can be modified. Changing the sequence of instructions is certainly one form of modification but the definition implies that a computer might somehow be able to modify its own instructions independently of those instructions. This is not quite true because an intermediate result must intervene, so there is some form of additional input into the machine that causes the modification. This can simply be thought of in terms of a feedback loop, wherein a process is continually modified by sensing the effect of its own actions (a thermostat for example). A computer can certainly modify its progress through a series of instructions by examining the effect of each step it makes, although such a feedback system must itself be subject to instructions. The definition is, however, unspecific and seemingly rather demanding, but computers, in principle, can modify their own software as a result of hardware and software interacting. Examples of this are found, particularly in 'artificial intelligence' research and in computers designed to 'learn'.

Computers, then, are general-purpose machines that can do anything that can be written down in the form of suitable instructions, providing that suitable hardware is available to implement those instructions. It is no good asking your desk-top micro-computer to give you white coffee unless it is attached to coffee-making apparatus. An individual machine may be quite specifically 'dedicated' to a particular task, such as making and serving coffee, and can still remain a computer. It is the notion of a computer which has been defined and no particular machine will, itself, be totally general-purpose.

Computers are conceptually very simple. Despite their technological sophistication (they are technically complex machines) they can only do a few things. What a computer does can be boiled down to just four functions. A computer can:

(1) Pass information between itself and the outside world.
(2) Store and move information around internally.
(3) Combine quantities together.
(4) Perform logical operations.

The first two of these functions concern nothing more than the transfer of information from one place to another and need no further comment. Combining quantities together, or adding, may seem a limited function but it means that all arithmetic operations can be performed by a computer, even though in principle it need only add. Multiplication can be performed by successive addition and there is a numerical method called 'subtraction by complement' that enables quantities to be subtracted by addition only. Hence division, which can be thought of as successive subtraction, can also be performed by a machine that can only add.

Computers can also make comparisons in the sense of following simple logical operations of the form represented by the words AND, OR, NOT. 'If x AND y then z', 'if x OR y then z' are typical statements that involve comparison in the sense that computers perform such a task. The combination of logical functions enables computers to obey a very wide range of possible instructions. Despite the apparent limitation of what computers can do, just four functions, they are nevertheless very versatile and efficient not least because those functions are supplemented by several other characteristics they possess.

To begin with, computers are fast. They can move inform-ation about and they can add and compare things very rapidly. Machine speeds are often discussed in terms of the number of additions that they can do in a second. A slow machine may only be able to perform a few hundred additions every second, a fast machine may perform several million in the same time.

Computers are also automatic machines, in that once they have been instructed to do something they accomplish the task automatically, without further human interference. Unlike a motor car, which needs continual human supervision in order to perform correctly, automatic machines, such as clocks and computers, just have to be set going and can then be left to themselves. Computers are also industrious, in that they will continue to obey instructions regardless of the length of time taken or the number of instructions to follow. Computers do not get tired, do not need holidays, will work day and night and they do not need to be paid, nor do they go on strike. Of course, they do need maintenance and they do require an electricity supply but, given those, a computer will work quickly, automatically and industriously. Whether you ask the machine to add ten numbers or ten million, it will obey your command and continue until the task is accomplished. It is perfectly possible to instruct a computer to continue doing something *ad infinitum* and it will repeat its task until you decide to stop it or turn it off.

Despite the fact that computers can only perform four basic operations they are, nevertheless, 'universal' machines in that they can be put to work on almost limitless tasks. Their versatility is high because the combination of the above characteristics of speed, industriousness and automatic operation with those four functions enables varied and complex tasks to be performed. All that is required, and it may not be as simple as it sounds, is for a desired objective to be reduced into simple operations that only require the four computer functions to come into play. The objective may be to model the earth's atmosphere, simulate the flight of an aircraft or do the necessary accounting to handle the payroll requirements of a large company. In all cases instructions need to be defined in the simple fashion that will enable the machine to carry them out. The versatility of the computer is achieved through the ingenuity of the written instructions, not from anything intrinsic in the machine itself.

One final characteristic of computers that should be mentioned is their precision. Computers will do precisely what they are instructed to do, providing their instructions are compatible with their capabilities. Even a basic pocket calculator will display the word 'Error' if it is asked to perform an illogical task, such as taking the square root of a negative number. If you ask a computer to add six to four, but inadvertently type in 'minus' for 'plus', then the answer given will be two instead of ten. The machine has done precisely what it was asked to do. Imprecisions do not occur unless the computer is in some way faulty, but if it is working fully then puzzling answers, wrong answers and other mistakes will be due, in general, to imprecise instructions or instructions that do not adequately express what the user intended. You may think you asked it to do what you wanted but the fault will lie either in the instructions or with the information that has been supplied with the instructions, and on which the latter are required to operate.

Computers, although precise, may not always be accurate. By this I do not mean that if you instruct a computer to add $2+2$ it will sometimes say 4 and sometimes say 3 or 5, because it is not very good at arithmetic. Computers will always be accurate in such a well defined case, but they may be less accurate in rather more subtle ways. For example the square root of 10 is 3.162; or is it? Certainly it is to three decimal places, but to four places its value is 3.1623 and to five places it is 3.16228. The square root of ten is not a simple fraction; like the square root of two, it is 'irrational', it cannot be represented by a simple ratio of two integer (or whole) numbers. In a computer such a number has to be approximated to, in the sense that it has to be 'rounded off' to so many decimal places, which will be determined by the size and complexity of the particular machine in question. I have used two pocket calculators, of which one was inexpensive and simple and the other more sophisticated and more expensive. If I take the square root of ten, both machines display the value 3.1622777. Taking the square root of that number gives 1.7782794 on both machines. If I then square the result and square it again I should end up with 10. One calculator displays 10.0000000 whilst the other reads 9.9999999. The cheaper machine gives a less accurate result (although it is only incorrect by 0.0000001) because it could not round off to as many places as the more expensive machine. Such errors, due to the way numbers are represented in a computer, can accumulate and therefore give inaccurate results, despite their precision.

Before condemning a machine for inaccuracy, however, the user should understand this limitation in handling numbers and work with data and results that are compatible in accuracy. The accuracy of the answer will depend on the accuracy of the weakest link in the series of operations being performed by the machine, and errors can accumulate in unhelpful ways in some calculations. In practice, the more sophisticated the computer system is the more likely it is that the results will be accurate, because techniques have been developed to overcome this problem. Despite this question of accuracy and error, computers are nevertheless precise and accurate in the sense of following rules and instructions correctly.

Having said that computers are conceptually simple machines, I now want to illustrate their structural simplicity (whilst acknowledging the complexity of their internal circuits etc.). Essentially, computers consist of just three parts, shown diagrammatically in Figure 1. These parts are a central processor, in which the computer operations are performed, which is linked to the other two: an input device and an output device. The central processor unit, or CPU in the jargon, is the real guts of the computer. The input and output devices are the links the computer has with the outside world. The input device may simply be a keyboard and the output device might be a visual display unit, such as a television set. The three things together form the complete system.

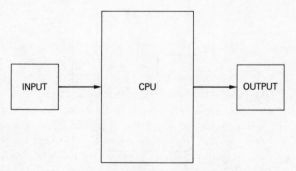

Fig. 1. Diagram showing elementary computer layout consisting of input, output and the central processing unit (CPU).

The central processing unit can be thought of as no more than a black box in which instructions are obeyed, but it is worth giving some details of its inner structure. The CPU itself consists of three essential areas, shown in Figure 2, namely the control section, the memory and the Arithmetic and Logic Unit (ALU). The control section, as its name implies, supervises the internal operation of the machine. It contains the instructions that are built into the machine, in contrast to those a user gives it to do some particular task. The control section is linked to most other parts of the computer and so 'knows' what state relevant parts of the machine are in. For example it monitors whether the line printer is free for printing or is being used, it 'knows' where programs have been stored in the memory, and so on. The control section supervises the performance of a particular job, it 'reads' the instructions, sends information to the places where it will be stored or processed, and does all the other 'housekeeping' tasks. Above all the control section ensures that the instructions are obeyed in the correct sequence.

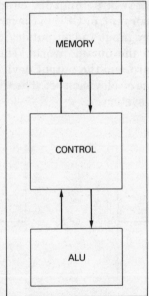

Fig. 2. The structure of the central processing unit, showing the control section, the memory and the arithmetic and logic unit (ALU).

The memory is that part of the machine where information, instructions and results are stored during the processing of a particular job. The memory, in the sense used here, is that part of the total storage space accessible to the machine that is physically inside it, in the CPU. It is internal memory in contrast to external memory, which may take the form of 'libraries' of magnetic tapes, magnetic discs, even punched cards or paper tape. Machine size is often referred to in terms of internal memory storage capacity. About one thousand characters (digits, letters and symbols) can be stored in 1K bytes of memory, where K stands for 1024 or 2^{10}. Computers are referred to as 8K, 32K or 64K machines in relation to the size of their internal memory, the storage space accessible directly to the control section during the operation of the machine and in which instructions, data and results must be stored.

This internal memory may be greatly extended by easily accessible external memory stores. Typical storage media are magnetic tapes and discs, punched cards and paper tape, all of which can be 'read' rapidly by the machine into its internal memory space. Small computers that are intended mainly for home use may be linked to an ordinary audio cassette player, so that instructions and data may be stored on cassette. The more expensive small computers use 'floppy discs' which are magnetic discs, not unlike thin gramophone records, and which can bend (hence floppy). Discs and cassettes can store an equivalent amount of data but discs are read much faster by the machine and are much more efficient. This is because the play-back head on the disc drive can move to any 'track' on the disc, whereas on a cassette the tape has to be run through to the part required. Large computers use both magnetic tape and magnetic discs on which large amounts of information can be stored (millions of characters) but of course large computers have correspondingly large internal memories.

The arithmetic and logic unit (ALU) is that section of the central processor where the adding and comparing of information takes place. This is the processing 'mill', as Charles Babbage originally called this unit in his pioneering work on computers in the nineteenth century. Numbers are sent to this unit from the memory, under the 'supervision' of the control section, to be added (subtracted, divided or multiplied) or to be compared. Arithmetic and logical operations are performed on information in this section of the computer.

The brief discussion of external memory also provides some indication of the form in which information can be put into a computer. Magnetic tape and disc drives, punched card and paper tape readers and so forth are all forms of input, when they are being 'read', although they can also be forms of output when information is being 'written' back on to tape, punched on card, etc. The keyboard or teletype terminal is the most obvious form of input but there are many other ways of putting information into a machine. A scanner, which 'reads' the black and white lines on library books or on tins of baked beans in the supermarket, is one way of reading into a computer. The electrical signal from a voltmeter, a digital thermometer or any other suitable instrument can be linked into the machine and is therefore a form of input in the same way as a microphone could be or a television camera. Switches or other sensing devices can also be computer input devices; in fact inputs can be found that correspond to sight, hearing, touch, even taste. Probes to monitor chemical reactions are used as computer inputs where the machine is, for example, controlling an industrial chemical process.

Similarly, output may be very varied and is certainly not confined to line printers and television monitors. The output may be the controlling mechanism of the cutting edge of a machine tool, the digital display of a watch, or a loudspeaker from which sounds can be produced to synthesize speech or music. The range is limited mainly by imagination and ingenuity. As I said earlier, computers no longer necessarily look like computers; their inputs may consist of buttons, electrically operated valves and thermostats, their outputs may consist of water flow and mechanical gyrations. The computer may look like a washing machine, but it is really a machine obeying an ordered sequence of instructions.

Figure 3 illustrates the interconnections of a complete computer system, showing how the control section is linked to all other units in order to be able to manipulate information in the system and to be able to monitor the functioning of all units. It will be noticed that external memory units can be both input and output devices, and that all inputs and outputs are directed

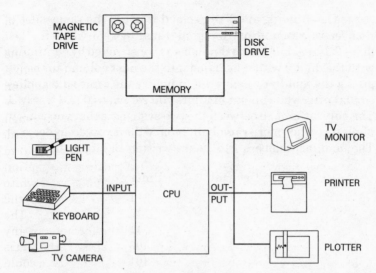

Fig. 3. Diagrammatic scheme of a complete computer system, showing various inputs, outputs and memory devices.

via the internal memory, the place where both data and instructions are stored whilst processing is taking place.

Having discussed the structure of the hardware, it is important, now, to say something of how it works before moving on to discuss software. As I said at the beginning of the chapter, the way computers work is essentially simple, even though the practical details are complicated. Computers are electrical machines and they work by passing electrical signals around their circuits, by combining electrical signals, and comparing electrical signals. The nature of those electrical signals is also simple, as far as the computer is concerned, in that by electrical signal is meant only the presence or absence of an electric or magnetic pulse. All that is then required is the supply of instructions and information which will be represented by the presence or absence of electrical pulses.

We are familiar with the decimal number system with its ten digits from 0 to 9, but number systems can be devised with any convenient number of digits. The simplest number system has only two digits, 0 and 1, and is called the binary number system. Binary, like decimal, can be used to represent any number by a sequence of digits, and like decimal it obeys the same rules of number representation. In the decimal system when the last digit, 9, is reached the next number is constructed by continuing with the digit 0 with a 1 carried into the next column to the left giving the familiar number 10. In binary the same rule applies, so that after you run out of digits you return to 0 and 'carry' 1. The only difference between the two systems is that you run out of digits rather more rapidly in binary than you do in decimal. The familiar numbers 1 to 10 are written in binary thus:

Decimal	Binary
1	1
2	10
3	11
4	100
5	101
6	110
7	111
8	1000
9	1001
10	1010

In decimal you begin a new column at every power of ten, that is at the number 10, 100, 1000, etc.; in binary a new column is begun at every power of 2, i.e. 2, 4, 8, 16, 32, 64, etc. to distinguish binary digits from decimal digits, binary digits are referred to as bits. Bits can be combined into 'words' and the size of 'word' a computer can handle depends on the particular machine in question. It may be anything from 2 bits to 64 bits long. The decimal equivalent of an 8-bit number would be about 500, which would be a rather limited range in most machines. A 60-bit number would give a range up to about 10^{18} (i.e. a million, million, million) in decimal, although much larger numbers can be expressed by using different forms of notation, but using the same number of bits.

Binary 'words' may be formed from 8-bit groups called bytes. Eight bits can be arranged in 512 different patterns so that each 8-bit pattern can represent the 10 decimal digits, the letters of the alphabet in both upper and lower case and still leave a large number of patterns for punctuation marks, mathematical symbols and so on. Hence words and numbers can be coded into binary notation using binary 'words' made up from 8-bit groups or bytes. For example, if the first 26 patterns (the binary form of the numbers 1 to 26) represent the letters A to Z, then the word 'WORD' would appear thus:

00010111	00001111	00010010	00000100
W	O	R	D

Each 8-bit pattern can then represent a character, and a full range of alphabetic and numeric characters can be incorporated into such a notation. The 0 bit can be represented by absence of electrical signal and the 1 bit by the presence of such a signal, so all information in the form of words and numbers can be handled by a computer in terms of presence or absence of electrical signals. Binary notation, the simplest form of 'language', provides the basis of the way a computer works.

Conveniently, electrical components such as transistors and their microtechnology equivalents (about which more in Chapter 3) can be used as logic gates, that is as components that electrically simulate logical operations. The three most elementary logic gates perform the logic operations AND, OR, NOT.

The AND gate gives an output of 1 (presence of signal) if both inputs are 1, that is 1 AND 1 gives 1, otherwise the result is 0:

The OR gate gives the result 1 if any input is 1, so the output will only be 0 if both inputs are 0:

Finally the NOT gate simply reverses the input:

There are more complex logic gates than these but the principle of operation is amply demonstrated by this selection. Circuit details and information about components can be found in suitable text books (see Further reading).

Binary arithmetic is simple, containing only four possible cases to deal with addition:

$$0+0 \text{ gives } 0 \text{ and carry } 0$$
$$0+1 \text{ gives } 1 \text{ and carry } 0$$
$$1+0 \text{ gives } 1 \text{ and carry } 0$$
$$1+1 \text{ gives } 0 \text{ and carry } 1$$

This could be reduced to only three possibilities as two of the cases given are equivalent. All these instances can be simulated electrically by a suitable arrangement of logic gates such as this example:

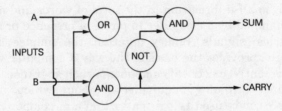

Fig. 4. An arrangement of logic gates combined to simulate addition.

If both inputs are 1, then 1 will result from both the OR and AND gates. The 1 from the AND gate will appear as the carry 1; it will also be reversed in the NOT gate so that there will be 0 and 1 inputs to the second AND gate and hence 0 as sum. The other variants can be worked through by the reader. This circuit does satisfy all the cases of binary addition.

By passing electrical signals around, maybe in groups of eight bits, and by passing them through circuits, like that shown in Figure 4, computers are able to carry out all the functions they are designed for and which can be manipulated into almost any conceivable application that can be written down as simple instructions.

Computers are simple machines in concept and yet the idea of writing instructions, solely in terms of 0s and 1s, that would enable a computer to work out income tax for several million people, seems very far from being simple. Instructions need to be expressed in a language and in computing there are not only different computer languages but also different levels of computer language. This hierarchical structure enables complex instructional problems to be made relatively simple, to the extent that people can pick up some elementary skills in instructing a computer to perform a simple task in quite a short time. A set of computer instructions is called a *program* and programming a computer can be done at different levels in the hierarchy.

At the deepest level in the machine, instructions must be in the form of binary digits, that is presence or absence of electrical signals. A machine needs to have a set of instructions built into it for the fundamental functions such as interpreting input signals, for moving bits around, for adding and comparing bits or bytes and for sending signals to output. These instructions are the integral functions of the central processor, and especially of the control unit. They are the signals that enable the machine to work.

One level up from these operating instructions are the manufacturer's machine codes. These are binary instructions that the machine is designed to interpret and obey. Although they may appear to be very basic instructions they will include multiple tasks that are 'understood' at the machine level. For example there may be a machine code for 'subtract', which will involve several operations in the central processor. Machine code programs belong to particular machines and manufacturers, and may be permanently built in to the machine or may be input to a machine when it is initially switched on.

It is possible with most machines for the user to write programs in machine code where each instruction will be in the form of a binary 'word', representing the nature of the instruction such as 'add', combined with an 'address' relating to the storage location to be collected from or delivered to. Computers come with handbooks listing the manufacturer's machine codes for a whole range of machine functions, which will be implemented by the operating instructions in the central processor.

An intermediate level in the hierarchy of 'languages' comes in the form of 'assembly language'. To make programming easier for the user, machine codes may be expressed by letters such as ADD, SUBT, MULT, DIV for the arithmetic functions, and which need to be converted into the binary codes of machine language, which can then be implemented by the machine. An instruction set, written in binary, called an *assembler* will translate input signals such as ADD or MULT into the appropriate binary machine code. This enables a programmer to write machine code instructions in a more accessible fashion without having to be constantly referring to a list of easily misread binary codes. We have seen that computers are fast and precise and are very suited to repetitive and monotonous tasks. Converting words into binary codes is just the sort of task they perform well, and this enables assembly languages to be designed.

High-level languages differ from those we have so far discussed in two ways. The languages and codes so far mentioned will be machine oriented, that is specific to a particular model of computer. High-level languages are general-purpose languages that can be understood, in principle, by any machine. Such languages are often designed to make programming easier for people tackling particular types of problem. Hence there are languages for business and accounting tasks, for scientific work and so on. High-level languages are also written to approximate as closely as possible to 'natural' language, such as English. In that sense they are extended versions of assembly language and they depend on the machine interpreting them into binary codes.

Although high-level languages try to emulate natural language they are very primitive forms of language, with rigid and precise grammatical rules. Mistakes over the placing of full stops or commas will lead to programs grinding to a halt, for at present computers cannot 'interpret' mistakes to any great extent. Nevertheless a computer program written in a high-level language should make some sort of sense to a person untrained in computer programming. For example, the following simple program should be readily comprehensible.

1. INPUT A
2. INPUT B
3. LET SUM = A + B
4. PRINT SUM

These instructions merely add together two numbers and print their sum, where the numbers would probably be input from a keyboard. The program does not specify what the numbers are, but represents them generally by labels which, in this case, are the letters A and B. In running such a program the user could type in 2, followed by 3 and the answer 5 would be output. Next time the program is run, or executed, to use the technical term, the numbers input could be 3647 and 8728 and the answer 12375 would be printed. The program itself is general in terms of its own scope; it will add any two numbers.

In order to use a high-level language a machine code program is required that translates the high-level language into the appropriate machine instructions. Such a translating program is called a compiler, because it compiles lines of program into sequences of machine instructions, or an interpreter, which is roughly equivalent. The compiler will either be input into the internal memory when the computer is operated or else it may be permanently held in the machine. Large computers may contain several compilers, so that different users may write their programs in different languages. Compilers do need to be machine specific, but the high-level language should be universal, at least in principle.

There are several hundred high-level languages around, many designed for quite specific application. The most well known and widely used languages are FORTRAN, ALGOL, COBOL and BASIC. The first two of these are best applied to numerical computation, whilst COBOL was designed for business and commercial applications. BASIC (which is an acronym for Beginners' All-purpose Symbolic Instruction Code) was designed as a simple, indeed a basic, form of high-level language, easy to understand, quick to learn, although not really efficient for more sophisticated or complex programming. In recent years languages like PASCAL, PL/1 and ALGOL68 have been developed that enable programs to contain powerful data and information structures that increase the 'naturalness' of the language and the efficiency and scope by which it can be implemented in a machine. Such languages are attempting to combine the advantages of many earlier languages and to advance the sophistication of general-purpose programming.

The software, that is the computer programs and the files of data to be processed, provide the specific tasks that the general-purpose computer hardware needs before it can be of any use. The program provides the sequence of instructions that the machine will obey. Running a program is termed its execution and can be accomplished once the program has been compiled.

In practice a source program, that is a set of ordered instructions written in a high-level language, will be input into the computer. Each line of instructions coming from the input device in the form of electrical signals (8-bit bytes) will be compiled, or turned into machine code instructions, and stored in the central processor memory. When all the program has been read, a command can be issued by the user to execute that program; the command (for example the word RUN) will be 'understood' by the control section, which will then pull the first instruction from the memory and obey its requirements. Then the second instruction will be obeyed and so on until the complete program has been run through. In the example program above, the first two instructions will involve the user in providing numbers which the control unit will have to fetch from input and store in the memory. The third instruction will involve sending number A to the ALU, then fetching number B, adding the two together and sending the sum back to a storage location in memory. The last instruction will require the sum to be sent from memory to the appropriate output channel. It seems a lot of work just to add two numbers but each stage of the process must be carried out precisely and in an orderly fashion. Computers are so fast in operation, however, that the complicated and fussy nature of their operating procedures is not an inconvenience to the user. Such speed has not always been possible; it has been achieved by technological advance, and that we now turn to.

3 CHIPS AND CHANGE

The computer was originally an idea ahead of its time. When Charles Babbage conceived of a universal computing machine in the second quarter of the nineteenth century the technology to build his *analytical engine* was just not available. In fact a hundred years had to pass before the first modern computers were built, and then they were slow, cumbersome and unreliable.

In 1944 the Harvard Mark I became the first modern computer, but its operation was not wholly electronic as part of its mechanism relied on cogs and wheels. In 1946, however, ENIAC was built and can claim to be the first all-electric computer. ENIAC stands for Electronic Numerical Integrator and Calculator. It weighed 30 tons, consumed 140 kilowatts of electricity, which presented enormous cooling problems, and it filled a very large room. ENIAC could add two numbers in one five-thousandth of a second and it consisted of around 18,000 vacuum tube valves. In the late 1940s several other valve-based computers were built but computing technology would not have progressed very far if the transistor had not been invented. When 18,000 valves were used in a computer like ENIAC there were daily valve failures, and the time taken to find the burned out component and replace it increased with the size of the machine. Even with ENIAC more time was spent looking for 'dead' valves than in running the computer so an alternative to the valve was required. Conveniently, in 1948 John Bardeen, Walter Brattain and William Shockley, at the Bell Telephone Laboratories, invented the transistor.

Computers are constructed essentially from switches. A switch can be on or off and so its state can represent a binary digit. By combining 'switches' in an electrical circuit the necessary units can be constructed to make a complete computer. The valves used in the earlier machines can be thought of simply as switches, and were often in the form of a diode. A diode is a device that passes an electrical current in one direction but not in the other. More complex valves were in fact used in the early computers but the principle remains the same. The transistor can do the job of a diode valve, in that it can pass an electrical signal or not, but it can also amplify a signal, making it stronger than before. This characteristic of transistors is very important. In other electrical components output signals are always weaker than the incoming signal, so to maintain a signal through a series of components the initial signal needs to be very strong or else it has to be boosted along the way. With transistors, however, weak signals can be perpetuated through several components without additional electric power. The heavy power consumption of valves is reduced dramatically in machines using transistors. Furthermore, transistors will act as controllable and nearly perfect switches.

Transistors are also *solid-state* devices; that is they are made of materials that can be combined in a solid unit to perform electrically as required. They have no moving parts but contain the properties they display within the characteristics of their material. Compared with the valve, they are far less susceptible to damage or to wear and tear, and they are far smaller. By the end of the 1950s valves had become obsolete and computers were firmly based on solid-state components, chiefly transistors.

The 1960s was a decade of consolidation and advancing sophistication in terms of refining the capacity, speed, efficiency and performing power of large computers. The year 1964 saw the Chilton Atlas installed at the Rutherford Laboratory in Oxfordshire. Built at the cost of one million pounds, the Atlas was the standard, in Britain at least, against which other computers were compared. It was housed in a two-storey building with the main frame of the machine at ground level and the input and output devices on the floor above. Atlas was fast, flexible and powerful. It was also large, expensive and rather inaccessible.

Transistors had made their impact not only through the efficiency of their design but also their compactness. During the 1960s the move towards further miniaturization was progressing and by the end of that decade the first micro-components, the first silicon chips, were being used. What they are will be discussed shortly, but the impact they had on computing technology was enormous. The idea of a chip is to build several electronic and solid-state components, like transistors, on the same piece of material. In this way components could be smaller and intrinsically connected to each other, hence doing away with pieces of wire, soldered joints and so on. The successive improvements in putting more and more components on to a single chip has led to the point where computers have almost disappeared. By this I mean that large main-frame computers, like the Atlas, are becoming things of the past, as their equivalent can now be packaged into a matchbox-sized unit. Computers are increasingly parts of other devices rather than machines on their own. The miniaturization of technology has transformed the computer world dramatically and very rapidly. Computers on chips have been made possible, not by major conceptual changes because the basic idea of a computer is still the same, but by rapid advances in technologies for designing and making chips from semi-conductor materials like silicon.

Metals, like copper and gold, conduct electricity because some of the electrons (the particles of negative electricity in the constituent atoms) in the material are so loosely associated to any particular atom that they can easily move about through the solid metal and hence carry an electrical current efficiently. Insulating materials, like carbon (for example, in the form of wood) or sulphur, have their electrons bound closely to each atomic nucleus so none are free to travel around and conduct electricity. Semi-conductor materials, such as silicon (the chief component of sand) and germanium, lie somewhat between the two extremes. Semi-conductors do not conduct electricity because their electrons are bound to the individual atoms in the material. However, some of those electrons are rather weakly bound and with quite a small 'push' they can be made to break loose and move through the crystal, hence conducting electricity. Semi-conductors conduct when induced to do so, for instance, by having a small electrical voltage applied across the material, of the magnitude expected in a component such as a transistor. In this way components made of semi-conductor material can be used as switches, because whether they conduct or not depends on the operation of the circuit. If a voltage is present then a current will flow and if no voltage is applied the current stops.

Materials like silicon can have their semi-conducting characteristics enhanced by being 'doped' with atomic impurities. If silicon contains a small amount of an element such as phosphorus, which has one more electron in its atomic structure than silicon has, then each extra electron donated by each impurity atom can move about freely, giving to this impure silicon enhanced semi-conducting properties. As the extra electron has a negative charge this type of impure silicon is called n-type. If silicon is 'doped' with an element such as boron, which has one less electron than silicon, then it acts as if an electron had been removed from the material or a positive charge had been put into it. This effective positive charge, caused by the absence of a negative charge, is referred to as a 'hole'. Positive 'holes' act, in the semi-conductor, just as effectively as a 'real' electrical charge would. This form of impure silicon is called p-type.

The combination of n-type and p-type silicon produces interesting electrical properties at their boundary which enable solid-state devices such as diodes and transistors to be made. In the simplest form a piece of p-type is joined to n-type silicon and a diode is produced. Current will flow from the p- to the n-type but not in the reverse direction. P-type silicon sandwiched between two sections of n-type creates a transistor.

These solid-state devices work entirely by the movement of electrons or positive holes under the influence of input electrical signals. They are solid: there are no moving parts except electric charges, and as they function at the atomic level the components can be made very small. Furthermore, these devices are very reliable as there is essentially nothing to go wrong with them unless they are damaged, for example by excess heat or a strong electrical surge. Once solid-state devices had been made and had replaced the cumbersome valve, then it was a natural progression to want to make the components smaller. Transistors, diodes and so on were originally discrete components, each having wires emerging from their plastic packaging and each having to be connected to the other components of a circuit. With the notion of increasing miniaturization came the idea of building several solid-state devices together in a unit, thereby eliminating the wire connections. This idea marked the beginning of chip technology.

As transistors are made from two types of doped silicon, and as diodes can likewise be made from silicon, the idea developed that, instead of making separate components, individual transistors and diodes could be made next to each other on the same piece of silicon material. By doping different parts of the same silicon substrate, or by applying thin coatings of different substances on one surface of a silicon wafer, suitable components could be embedded on the single base. The technology to do this had to be refined but the basic idea was not complicated. Figure 5 shows the sort of arrangement envisaged. The different parts could then be connected by layers of aluminium conductor coated on to the silicon wafer in such a pattern as made the connections necessary to complete a desired circuit. As the wafers used are small they rapidly became known as chips.

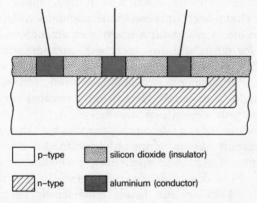

p–type

silicon dioxide (insulator)

n–type

aluminium (conductor)

Fig. 5. Diagrammatic view of a section through a silicon wafer on which has been built a section of n-type silicon, silicon dioxide insulator and aluminium connectors.

Part of the technology in making micro-electronic components on chips involves the process of evaporating thin coatings of substances on to the surface of the substrate. The coatings might be insulating materials, such as silicon dioxide, or they might be metallic conductors. Thin-film technology was well enough developed to have this potential and it enabled circuit designers to incorporate into their planned circuits on chips such customary components as resistors and capacitors. A standard resistor is made from a poorly conducting material that resists the passage of electricity through it. Such a component could be produced on a chip by embedding a thin wedge of one type of silicon in a substrate of the opposite type. A capacitor standardly stores electricity between plates of conducting material. The micro equivalent of a conventional capacitor can take the form of a layer of conducting metal coated on top of a layer of insulating material over the silicon base. By embedding different impurity types of silicon into a silicon substrate, and by making successive surface coatings, a whole range of components, including their interconnections, can be assembled as one solid-state and very small unit.

The process of combining components together on a single chip of silicon is referred to as integration and the first integrated circuits on chips were produced in the mid-1960s. Since then, as will be discussed shortly, more and more components have been squeezed on to the space available on a chip, which measures about a quarter of an inch square. The technique for doing this involves both photographic etching and thin-film technologies, which in themselves have needed considerable refinement and sophistication, but which yet remain simple in principle. The other technical requirement was for very pure crystals of silicon.

Integrated circuits on silicon chips are made in this way. First of all the circuit has to be not only designed but designed in three dimensions. As the components are constructed in layers, each layer of the design needs to be carefully drawn and the relationships between the levels considered. The designed circuit is then drawn accurately on a large scale, where each picture represents regions where silicon or other material will be either coated on or removed from that level. The drawings are then photographically reduced until they form minute photographic masks.

During this design process a large crystal of pure silicon will be manufactured. This is normally cylindrical and may be a foot or two in length. The crystal will then be sliced up into thin disc-shaped wafers, each of which will eventually contain several hundred chips. The wafers will next be coated with silicon dioxide and then covered with a special photographic emulsion called photoresist. At this point the wafers and the photo-graphically reduced masks come together. Light is shone through the mask and 'exposes' those parts of the photoresist that it reaches. This is really the same process as in normal photography. The chemical properties of the emulsion alter on exposure to light so that, when the wafer is subsequently placed in a bath of a suitable chemical, the exposed part remains whilst the unexposed part is removed by the wash. The wafer is then placed in an acid solution which etches away the silicon dioxide exposed by the removal of the photoresist. The underlying silicon is thereby exposed to view in that place and can have impurities embedded in it or layers of conductor or other material coated on to it. Another chemical wash will then remove the remaining photoresist and one layer of the chip is complete. By continuing this process over several layers, complex patterns of circuit components can be built together on the wafer.

Finally the wafer will be sliced into the separate chips, for the patterns implanted on to the silicon will have been manifold. The individual chips are then electronically tested to see whether they work and finally mounted in a plastic case ready for use. Even small defects at what is virtually the atomic level in the material can spoil a chip but, as so many are made on one wafer, spoilage is not too important. Indeed technical improvements in chip manufacture have led, in recent years, to high yields of good chips from each wafer.

The early chips contained just a few components and replaced parts of electronic circuits. By the end of the 1960s chips contained several hundred components and the advances that led to this improvement gave rise to the phrase Large Scale Integration. With hundreds or even a few thousand components on a chip, central processing units could be contained on one piece of silicon, giving rise to the word *microprocessor*. Chips were made with arrays of transistors that could be used for storing data or programs and which therefore acted as memories. These came in two sorts, ROM and RAM. ROM (Read Only Memory) chips are made with instructions or data built into them; for example they may contain the interpreter for a high-level language like BASIC. The information can be retrieved from such a memory but new information cannot be stored. The memory is permanent. Random Access Memory allows both reading and writing into the storage locations and the random access means that the machine can turn to one location as easily as any other. The memory does not have to be read in sequence. The Write Only Memory has never been successfully developed!

It became possible in the mid-1970s, therefore, to build a small computer by using just a handful of suitable chips; one for the central processor, including the arithmetic and logic unit, a second to interpret the signals from the keyboard, maybe another interfaced to the TV monitor output. A few more chips could be used for memory and a system could be packaged in a desk-top box not much larger than a conventional office typewriter. Such a machine could have the processing capability of an appreciable fraction of the Chilton Atlas and for about a thousandth of the price. The new micro-computers were fast, cheap and very accessible.

Large scale integration gave way to VLSI, Very Large Scale Integration. The year 1975 saw the development of the 64K chip: a single sliver of silicon containing over 64 thousand bit locations, or the equivalent number of components for a powerful central processor and arithmetic and logic unit. Such a development led to the notion of 'the Chilton Atlas in a pocket', but the progress continued. Before the end of the 1970s the million-bit chip had been produced, together with the concept of a whole computer on a chip. At the time of writing, chips have been announced with as many as four million components squeezed on to them. Figure 6 illustrates this dramatic change in what has become technically feasible.

The limit to packing yet more components on to a silicon chip lies not so much in the space available on the wafer but with the ability to reduce designs photographically. The next development, therefore, is to turn away from photographic procedures completely and operate on the chip with a beam of electrons. Such a technique, whereby etching the chip surface can be much more finely accomplished, enables an increase of between a hundred and a thousand times the number of components to be fitted together. The electron beams would be guided under computer control and the chip design would be programmed into the computer. Computer developments therefore enhance

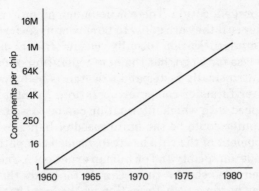

Fig. 6. Graph showing the increase in the number of components that can be placed on a chip from 1960 until around 1980.

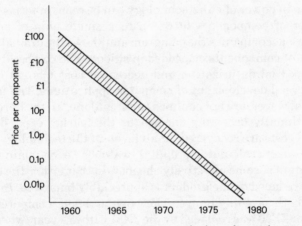

Fig. 7. Graph showing the decreasing cost of micro-electronic components since the early 1960s.

their own design and manufacture, accelerating their progress still further. Such developments are currently in progress and chip capacity will continue to increase in the next few years.

Alongside VLSI are other technical advances in the production of memory chips. Devices based on components other than transistors (the so-called charge-coupled devices and magnetic bubbles) are being introduced which may not only increase memory size but which also increase access time to any particular storage location. There is not much point in making computers bigger if they are going to be slower in performance. Of course, miniaturization usually means faster, because signals have less far to go, but the new generation of memory devices are intrinsically faster and research is being pursued into still faster forms of computer operation. Eventually the limit to the speed with which information can be passed around inside a computer could be the finite speed of light.

The development of the chip has transformed computing but it has also made, on society and on human experience, an impact unprecedented in so short a time span. In ten years the micro revolution has begun a transformation whose force has barely been felt and the implications of which are the subject matter of this book. Figure 6 is one of two graphs that illustrate, in a simple and direct fashion, the force of this revolution. There, the rise in power of chip technology can be seen, in terms of the number of components fitted on to a single chip of silicon. Figure 7 accompanies that diagram and shows the dramatic fall in cost of components embedded in silicon. The combination of increased miniaturization and decreased cost has led to the widespread development of computer applications. The falling costs, however, are not confined to chips alone; all the hardware is continually becoming cheaper as the market expands and capital costs are recovered. At all levels of the technology costs fall. Pocket calculators, digital watches, even main-frame computers become effectively cheaper, in that either the direct cost is reduced or the product is appreciably improved. In some cases both factors change. The popular home computer, the Sinclair ZX80 was replaced by the ZX81 within a year, where the later model was a considerably improved version and its cost had fallen by 30 per cent. Similar stories are associated with other machines, with TV monitors, line printers and other accessories, but it is in the area of multiplying applications that the cost effectiveness of chip-based microprocessors has had most effect and which has led to public awareness of the revolution in our midst. The scope of those applications is the subject matter of the next chapter but before that is approached one more technical matter should be discussed, namely how a microprocessor can be linked to the outside world.

Computers are digital machines. They work by processing digital information and they 'communicate' by signals in the form of binary digits. Digital information is information expressed in numbers, in a purely quantitative fashion. In the world arounds us most information is found in analogue form. Analogue information is information expressed as a physical analogy of the original quantity. For example temperature is normally expressed in analogue form by the height of a column of mercury in a glass tube. When you read a thermometer you are examining how much the liquid has expanded or contracted in that tube and you express that height as if it were temperature. When we read a thermometer what we actually do is perform the mental process of converting the physical analogue of temperature into so many degrees, that is into a digital form. Any physical quantity that changes with temperature can be used as a thermometer, however, and the electrical properties of certain conductors can be used as analogues of temperature. Electrical analogues can easily be converted into digital form by a suitable small electronic circuit (A–D converter) and the temperature can then be expressed on an electrically driven digital display; that is, it will appear as a number such as 21.4°C. Such a display can be read directly, so eliminating the mental process required for analogue forms.

Time is traditionally expressed in analogue form by falling sand in an hour-glass or by a pendulum-driven pointer, whose angular relationship with a dial indicates the time. Recently, digital watches have invaded the analogue market and many people now read the time directly in terms of numbers. Any signal that can be converted into an electrical form can be passed through an analogue-to-digital converter and then presented in digital form. Conversely digital information can go through a digital-to-analogue converter and be expressed in analogue form, such as by a pointer against a dial, the strength of an electrical voltage or by the motion of a cog or wheel.

In terms of a computer these conversion processes are usually necessary for input and output channels. The electrical signal generated when touching a key on a keyboard has to be turned into a binary signal, which will be in the form of, for example, a train of eight pulses (or their absence). If the binary form of the signal for the letter W is 00010111 then a pulse train may appear thus:

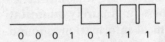

$$0 \quad 0 \quad 0 \quad 1 \quad 0 \quad 1 \quad 1 \quad 1$$

Inside the computer this digital signal will be moved about and processed in the ways discussed above but, when the letter W is to be printed on the TV monitor screen or on a printer, the signal has to be converted back into a form that results in its analogue appearing as the pattern of light (or ink) on the screen (or paper) in the shape W. The circuits that convert information about the world outside the black box of a computer into binary digits and vice versa are described as the interfaces with the computer. The power and flexibility of computers in their application depends partly on man's ingenuity in turning *any* information into electrical form, which is thence converted to a binary code, but partly on a computer's processing ability.

An analogue wrist-watch and a digital one are similar in that both display information on their faces about the time. They do this by converting the periodic oscillations of an escapement wheel or a quartz crystal into a changing display, but the main difference between them is that the digital watch can also process the information and store it. The digital watch is a simple computer, based on one silicon chip. Its input comes in the form of regular electrical pulses from the battery-driven oscillating quartz crystal, its output is the display on its face. Whereas the conventional watch mechanically converts oscill-ations to moving hands, the digital watch processes inform-ation. In addition to displaying the time, the watch will be able to store the current time in a memory location—indeed it does this as a fundamental operation, outputting the current time to display every second from that store. The watch can usually be switched to display a stored date from another memory location. This date is corrected daily according to instructions stored elsewhere and which should include data on the length of months and even when leap years occur. The same input signals can also be operated on to provide a stop-watch mode of operation or to store time signals for other places in the world. Times can be stored so that an alarm noise can be generated and so on. All these functions can be provided out of just the same input information as supplies a conventional watch. The ability to perform these different applications comes purely from the computer's ability to process information.

There is one other aspect of the interfacing of computers to the outside world which must be mentioned and which is becoming increasingly important and that is the subject of information communication. Communications technology, much of it chip-based, is proliferating and advancing as rapidly as micro-computing. Indeed the two things are both aspects of microtechnology and mutually dependent.

Computers process information very rapidly and move data internally at great speed. Even small machines can process ten million bits every second and yet conventional communications media are very much slower. A typewriter can only be operated at a few bits per second and a telephone line can only carry information at a rate of around a thousand bits per second. Such links are far too slow, particularly if computers are linked to each other in a network of information exchange. In recent years, communications cables, the same as used for carrying television programmes, have become far more widespread and these cables carry a million or more bits every second. Optical fibres (thin strands of glass or similar material) carry a thousand million bits in a second and are now being developed technically for communications networks. In the USA particularly, but also elsewhere in the world, communications satellites are increasingly transferring information at rates of ten or more million bits per second, so that data transmission technology is catching up with machine processing speeds. The ability to interlink computers in this way is greatly extending their power and the range of their potential application. Linked computers processing information and being interfaced both to one another and to a comprehensive range of digital and analogue devices has led to the widespread application of computing technology, to the invasion of the chip.

4 THE TRANSFORMATION OF TECHNOLOGIES

When technology becomes the input and output of a processor on a chip its whole nature is changed; that is the power of the micro revolution. The miniaturization of computing hardware has enabled that processing power to be embedded in virtually any and every other technology, hidden from sight, yet surreptitiously changing the nature of the machinery it has taken control of. The decreasing cost of chips has meant that applications of computer control now range from the most sophisticated to the utterly trivial, whilst the growth of communications networks spreads that control not only around the country but also around the world. The invasion of the chip has taken the form of an infiltration and it is only now, when the effects of the take-over are beginning to be noticed, that we realize that the chip is with us and around us.

There are so many applications of chip technology that it would be monotonous to list them all. However, in this chapter, I shall look at five main areas in which microtechnology has already had a great impact, choosing examples in each area to illustrate the way a microprocessor changes other technologies. We have already seen how a watch is transformed when its source of oscillations becomes an input to a processor and its 'face' becomes the output. It then ceases to be a watch but becomes a time processor! This kind of transformation can be seen in all aspects of *machine control*, which is the first area of applications we turn to.

Consider a machine tool consisting of a cutting edge for shaping a piece of metal, a clamp to hold the metal and a series of control handles to enable the operator to manipulate the work-piece and the cutting edge. The operator performs a series of actions bringing the cutting edge to the right place on the metal, in the right orientation, and uses the cutter until that part of the work is done. Then the metal may be reoriented and further work done on it, maybe with a change of cutting tool.

Apart from any manual skills involved, the operator has to judge the extent to which the work is being correctly accomplished, see if there is ample lubricant and coolant flowing, and so on. The process can be performed automatically, for example on a production line, by having a machine mechanically controlled to cut or drill on a piece that is placed in front of it. This kind of human replacement in a workshop may relieve an operator of repetitive work and provide a uniform product but such a system is expensive to set up and very inflexible. Furthermore the cutting edge will do its task whether or not there is a metal sample in front of it and regardless of whether the work-piece is faulty or not. The machines blindly perform their automatic task.

When a machine tool becomes interfaced to a processor it is transformed. It is nothing like the automatic line of machines, nor is it very like a tool in a human hand. To a manufacturer it has all the 'advantages' of the human operator (flexibility, 'judgement', ability to monitor, etc.) with none of the 'disadvantages' (becoming bored, inaccurate, tired, hungry or going on strike). The processor takes control and transforms the machine tool. Its inputs are its instructions, the program for the job in hand, as well as various sensors that it uses to judge position (microswitches), temperature (thermocouples), lubricant flow, etc. Its outputs are the movements of the cutting edge (or edges, as it can be built with multiple tool heads for drilling, milling, cutting, maybe simultaneously) and signals to indicate its progress to the operator and to other machines.

The automated machine tool becomes a system of its own. Its job can be changed simply by a change of program. It can monitor its job as it goes, stopping if the work-piece is faulty. It can work on several operations at the same time, making itself much more efficient than a human operator and it can monitor itself and its supplies whilst it works. Linked to other machines and other parts of a work place it can order itself more coolant or lubricant as its supply gets low, it can also report on how the work is progressing to the factory manager, accountant, storeman and maintenance department. The machine tool with a chip is a different order of machine, it has become a processor of metal.

With such machines, manufacturing itself is transformed

from a series of processes that largely involve the manufacture of specific objects to a system of information flow, where the product can become almost irrelevant. What is important in the automated factory is information flow to the machines and from the machines, which themselves are a link in the actual business of the undertaking. Chip-controlled machines interfaced to a small central computer can run the factory, only needing supervision and maintenance, although even servicing may be diagnosed by the machine itself and involve the engineer merely in exchanging faulty parts for new ones. The machines doing the manufacturing can supply management directly with information and can be linked to a larger computer which itself may be analysing business planning and development alternatives for management decision. The machine tool as a system, as a machine that 'thinks', becomes part of a larger system in which the whole industrial process is computer controlled. It does not matter whether the system is an industrial chemical plant or a steel works or a factory making ballpoint pens, when the machine tools become controlled by a chip-based processor not only is the machine transformed but the process of which it is part.

The high-technology industries, the businesses based on electronic products, are already semi-automated; heavy manufacturing is beginning to become so, as instanced by Fiat car production in Italy. Automation is an emotive subject and has been so for far longer than real automation has been with us. The dangers and benefits of machine control were worried about and discussed from the 1930s onwards, although pure automation is only emerging seriously fifty years on. The social and human impact of such a process we shall discuss in later chapters; now we return to the transforming effect of the chip on other technologies.

The notion of machine control can be extended from the industrial process into every aspect of technology. The combination of information-processing capacity and suitable environmental sensors (e.g. thermometers, pressure gauges, flow meters, etc.) can result in machines monitoring themselves for optimum performance and diagnosing their state of repair. The car with a chip under the dashboard can regulate its own fuel consumption by adjusting fuel injection to driving conditions.

By displaying instantaneous fuel consumption a car can 'advise' its driver to drive more economically. It can monitor the state of the brake and hydraulic fluids, it can 'watch' oil consumption and electrical performance, 'suggesting' to the owner when the car needs servicing and what needs checking. The car can become transformed around the chip, providing the driver with a vast range of information and advice. It still has to be driven from A to B but with the development of suitable distance sensors the car could itself apply brakes when being driven too fast or too close to other objects for safety. Given a communications link the car could also 'talk' to the garage, booking itself in for a service or a road test, applying for its own road tax and insurance and merely notifying its owner it had done so. The car itself becomes an information-processing machine.

Computing technology developed from military applications and has been furthered for military ends rather more than for civil purposes, which is generally the case with technologies. The cruise missile and other chip-controlled weapons are transformations of orthodox methods of killing. The 'intelligent' bullet, as the cruise missile has been called, is not aimed at a target but sent to find its own. It can be programmed with a list of targets, with priorities for their destruction; the missile is launched with built-in maps of the terrain over which it needs to travel. It flies low above the ground, sensing its position and its path, detecting where the land lies around it, where there are trees and buildings to avoid. It can detect counter-attacking missiles and take avoiding action of its own, determined to reach the optimum target on its list depending on what it encounters on its way. Computers were initially designed to help aim artillery weapons accurately; they have been developed to the extent that a missile can contain tens of processors on chips, working to help guide the missile's destructive power on to a target of its own choice.

More than this, the missile can process visual information if fitted with a suitable television camera. When it finds its target, a tank or a ship, it can circle its prey 'looking' for what it has been programmed to detect as the target's weakest spot. No more random firing at an enemy, now the bullets stalk their victims, working out how best to kill. The missile may also be linked to spy satellites high in the upper atmosphere, whose electronic eyes send their pulsed signals to larger computers that interpret what is being seen, finding troops or vehicles by the heat they give off despite their disguised positions. The satellite watches like a hawk, the missile strikes.

The control of the machines of war by computers has its logical extension into the electronic battlefield, first introduced by the United States forces in Vietnam. Electronic surveillance of the territory is carried out by satellites and by ground-based sensors that can distinguish between vehicle movement and human footsteps. Weapons, perhaps prearranged and embedded in the countryside, may be triggered by the electronic detectors, choosing via their logic gates which weapons to aim at what targets. Missiles will be guided by the surveillance computers and helicopter gun ships can be navigated to the most effective place to rain down fire on enemy personnel entering the electronically controlled lands. In addition, like the factory machine, the computer-linked weaponry can pass back information to a central computer where strategies can be modelled, based on exactly what is occurring on the battlefield, and logistics can be ordered according to current needs. Success in war can then depend on information flow.

Not unconnected with warfare is space research and exploration. The Apollo project to the moon and subsequent spacecraft exploring the planets all ride on the rocketry used to launch military satellites both in the USA and in the Soviet Union. These projects depend heavily on miniaturized computers and micro-electronics generally, and although their payloads are scientific, it is unlikely that governments would invest the amounts of money and manpower into them that they do just for the excitement of finding out about the atmospheric gases on Jupiter.

From machine control we turn to *science and research* as the second main area of microtechnology applications and here, space research epitomizes the use of the chip and of chip-based communications systems. Pictures of the distant planets have been transmitted from spacecraft in the form of binary digits output by the craft's computer after the television images have been processed into transmittable form. Back on earth those signals are reprocessed and the crude images 'improved' by computer techniques. Computer graphics techniques are sufficiently well developed nowadays for colours to be enhanced, edges 'smoothed' and ambiguous parts of an image clarified. Indeed, graphics can now be generated that simulate, on a two-dimensional screen, three-dimensional objects, built up from sets of instructions about shape, form, surface, colour and shading. The graphics need no longer remain stationary for their animation is now standard practice.

In scientific research similar techniques may be employed to model the structures of complex molecules before laboratory synthesis is attempted of a new pharmaceutical drug. Astrophysicists can manipulate graphically whole galaxies of stars or compress the evolution of the universe into a few seconds on their computer terminal screens. Any dynamical situation in physics, chemistry, engineering or even mathematics can be constructed in graphical form by a computer. In engineering and research, computer-assisted design is now often regarded as a necessity, a prerequisite for successful work.

Computers as calculating machines are mainly the province of science and technological research. To analyse the light from a star or study the structure of a crystal requires enormous computing capacity, vast numbers of calculations, but the application of the chip affects science in much smaller but nevertheless transforming ways. Just as the machine tool has been invaded by the chip so have scientific instruments. Apart from the flood of instruments with digital displays which do not differ in principle from the watch there are other ways in which instruments have been transformed. The example I present concerns something very simple, a voltmeter.

A colleague of mine added a microprocessor to a voltmeter used by a geologist. Formerly the geologist had gone on a field trip, maybe to a remote site, and drilled into the rocks of interest to him. The thin wire probe used, sensed small electrical changes at different depths through the rocks and these signals appeared as voltages on a simple meter. That information could then have been written down by hand as columns of numbers but was in fact passed through a digitizer and into a punch, which converted the experimental data into holes in a punched paper tape. The tapes obtained on the field trip were then taken back to the university and fed into the main-frame computer. Eventually the data was analysed and yielded the information being sought. Sometimes the data was faulty or insufficient and another field trip would be arranged.

A voltmeter with a chip was a different thing altogether; now the geologist could probe his rocks and the voltages obtained could be stored on a chip and processed on the spot. The outcome of the experimental work could be presented to him then and there just because his instrument had some processing capacity. The efficiency and usefulness of the device was transformed.

New scientific applications depend on chip technology. The space probes are typical of devices for exploring hostile environments which would be quite unsuitable for man to venture in, at least without great cost and risk. New instruments can be conceived which could not work without computer speeds. For example electronic light detectors used in astronomy require thousands of signals to be 'read' every second or even every millionth of a second. Such speeds in manipulating information were inconceivable before silicon-based technology was invented.

In medicine, as in all areas of scientific research, the chip brings new tools into play. Information-processing instruments not only give faster and, frequently, more reliable results in laboratory tests but such devices can also monitor and control a whole experimental arrangement. They can even monitor the condition of several patients, advising central nursing or medical personnel of their patients' progress. Medical diagnosis is also being developed in more sophisticated ways but I will do no more than mention that topic here as we return to it later in the book.

In applied science, in industrial laboratories, quality control and product testing is increasingly being taken over by chip-based machines which can not only test products during manufacture but also adjust the manufacturing process itself if the product fails to maintain its required standard. Indeed the chip monitors its own manufacture and is used to test new chips as they are produced on silicon wafers. Chip-based products are constantly being developed and so microtechnology changes the nature of industry as well as of industrial processes.

The third broad area of microtechnology and computing applications is that of *information processing*; this differs from the first two in that whereas machine control and scientific applications involve transformed hardware, with information processing it is that nebulous entity 'information' which is the product. Of course information is being processed in all computer applications because that is what computers do and the five distinctions between the different areas I am presenting are little more than ones of taste; however, I suggest information processing is distinct from machine control, at least in terms of product and of human activity. It is the area in which computers have always made great impact and through which they are most familiar.

I am going to say little about large information systems such as payroll, income tax or car registration systems. This type of information processing is generally well known and most large organizations, government agencies, banks and insurance companies have personnel records, payroll and business information, accounts, etc. on computers. Such systems are referred to as data-base systems as they consist of a large bank or base of information or data which is manipulated in the computer according to the requirements of the user. Such data-base systems may be used for calculating company accounts or for business or government statistics. Such information systems, whilst improved by new developments in both hardware and software in recent years, have not been directly affected, at least in principle, by microtechnology as such except in two respects. Firstly, falling prices of memory devices have enabled even small organizations to afford an information system and secondly, as mentioned in other contexts, microtechnology has enabled local and international communications networks to expand greatly. One consequence of this has been that computers are now easily linked to other computers, which means that data-based systems can, in theory at least, be extended between many machines and accessed by small computers that can be plugged into the network, maybe by telephone lines. Such a development not only extends the data base and its use but means that data bases can be combined or that information processing can be operating on a vast network and not just locally. The international airline booking system is the most obvious example of such a network and it is not easy to imagine how international flights could be efficiently organized without a computer-based and communications-linked system. As chip-based communications channels proliferate and the occurrence of computers 'talking' to computers becomes commonplace not only will great flexibility be introduced into networked systems but also many problems will arise which will be discussed in Chapters 8 and 9.

Information processing is often associated with the so-called office revolution which is taking place as chip-controlled machinery invades offices of all sorts. Word processors are replacing conventional typewriters and filing systems and, as a result, replacing typists and filing clerks. A word processor consists of a keyboard, a television screen and a microprocessor, usually combined with one or two floppy disc drives and output to a printer. Text can be typed on the keyboard, displayed on the screen and stored on a disc. Recalled text can be edited, either to remove errors or to alter for a different use and can then be printed out. A typical example might consist of a standard letter inviting someone to visit your office. Each time an invitation is sent the letter can be re-edited changing the addressee's name, the date and so on but leaving the main text unaltered. Such a system saves much typing time, saves space, and time searching for files, because the machine looks for you. Mailing lists can be stored, coded in such a way that selective mailing can take place to people in pre-arranged categories. The word processor can then match the names to the circular so that each one seems personal; it prints out the envelopes as well. As printing speeds are very rapid and machines can operate continuously, the use of a word processor can transform secretarial practice.

The office revolution does not stop there, however, for basic text editing, automatic filing and the merging of text with name and address files are only the start. As a word processor is effectively a computer terminal there is no reason why it should not be linked to other word processors or word-processing terminals. In such an office network system, internal mail can be sent automatically in the form of digital signals that are moved around the system and stored in the files of the receiver's terminal. When switching on a terminal the user can look in the 'mail-box' to see if messages have been left there. No paper is passed around at all. The same can be done with any 'document' that has been generated or stored in a word processor. Offices are beginning to do away with that kind of paper.

Electronic mail can, of course, be extended beyond the network of a particular office system. By use of communications links, either by telephone line or cable system (even by radio and satellite link), one office can be interfaced with other places that have compatible machines. Then no letters need be sent physically at all; mail will become the transfer of electrical signals from one computer terminal to another. Already televisual 'conference' links have been set up, where executives can talk to and see each other in different locations to avoid the expense and inconvenience of travel. Electronic mail will also link businesses and agencies in a new and probably closer relationship as computer-based information can travel rapidly and in large quantities. Naturally the office terminal could be linked to larger computers and hence used for putting information into a data base or for interrogating such a system in order to gain relevant information.

The office terminal extends beyond being a word processor, it is transformed into an information centre. By choosing the appropriate link a secretary at a terminal can book airline tickets, obtain reports from other personnel, send memos, check up on invoice queries, arrange timetables for staff holidays and obtain stock exchange prices or weather reports. The electronic office will certainly make use of view-data types of information service, giving office personnel access to countless commercial and official information services.

The secretary with a word processor becomes a computer operator of sorts, certainly in the sense of interacting with a microprocessor-based system. Like any computer user, the secretary will almost certainly fall under its spell, finding the man–machine interaction hypnotic, captivating and compelling. Computers bring out the hacker in us all as we manipulate the system and are manipulated by it in turn. The more powerful the software and the system the more compelling the terminal becomes and the more the operator is inclined to use and even extend its facilities to the full. At the same time skills change or are taken over by the machine. The typist no longer needs to take care over the presentation of the typed page, the machine does that automatically, justifying the margins, centring the headings, even hyphenating words that need to be split at the end of a line. Word processors may be equipped with a 'dictionary' and can compare typed words with those correctly spelled in the store, indicating where a typist has made a mistake and might like to alter what was typed. Typing speeds increase on a word processor as the machine takes over many of the physical processes and indeed typing itself is transformed; words only appear on a screen until the final, edited text is ready for printing.

Chip-based printers obtain signals from a disc or other storage source and translate those signals as commands to a printing head. Many computer-linked printers create alphabetic and numerical characters by a series of dots or lines not unlike a digital display on a watch. For office-quality typing, word processors usually have printers with the type arranged radially on a plastic disc with each letter at the end of a stem so the whole arrangement looks like a daisy—the daisy wheel printer. In operation the disc spins rapidly and the required character is imprinted by being struck by a key much like that in an ordinary typewriter only faster. Typical printing speeds may be a hundred characters per second although the printer will store whole sections of text which it can receive from the word processor at much faster transfer rates.

Typewriters are, of course, only one form of printing device and microtechnology has transformed other printing machinery as well. Traditional printing was set up in blocks using cast metal characters but modern typesetting has replaced metal type by photographic methods. A modern photo-typesetting machine incorporates a set of printing characters usually in digital form. The characters are generated by means of a special screen and transferred optically to photographic film. By passing the image through a set of lenses, the size of the character as it appears on the film can be altered at will. A complete page of print can be set in this fashion. Developed film then yields a master sheet of the print from which the litho plates will be made for multiple printing. Such machines are chip-based so that type can be set very rapidly.

The logical extension of such a photo-typesetting machine is to interface it with a word-processing system and then the output of the text-editing process can be set in the printing type face but produced as easily as normal typing. In this way a typist can become transformed into a printer and the printing industry left without a function. In the newspaper business, such machinery has caused extensive management and labour difficulties as, in principle, a journalist can sit at a terminal and hammer out his story. The electronic file with the item can be transferred to a sub-editor to edit the piece and the editor can place it where he thinks fit on the page. A single press of a key on a keyboard and the news item is then automatically typeset and is ready for printing, bypassing several orthodox processes. Indeed a one-man newspaper is now quite feasible because the technology enables all the different tasks to be performed on one machine.

The automated office, especially as it becomes linked with other offices and other information networks, becomes transformed not just physically, with the abolition of the filing cabinet, but also in its function. The orthodox office serviced an organization, fulfilled functions required by managers, but the silicon office processes information, it becomes central to the transactions of the organization because information becomes the prime product. In this sense information itself is transformed by the chip and an example in a slightly different area will explain this point more clearly.

One form of information processing is used by banking where the combination of bank computers and rapid communications networks is transforming not just accounting but the whole question of money, its use and transfer. When I am paid my salary I receive a note from my employer printed by a computer telling me how much I have earned each month, how much tax has been deducted and so on. The money has been transferred to my bank account and I don't see it, at least not as bank notes, unless I cash a cheque for it at my local bank. My employer's bank has electronically transferred funds from its account to mine. There is nothing unusual about this at all.

Such a scheme can and is being extended to enable normal cash transactions to be performed in the same way, that is by computer communication rather than by handing over cash from one person to another. The scheme, referred to as EFT

(Electronic Funds Transfer), is not the same as having a credit card, which requires monthly accounting, but operates rather like salary payment. A visit to a supermarket for groceries would end up with your personal 'chip-on-a-card' being 'read' by the 'cash register' and the money owed would automatically be transferred from your bank account to that of the shop. Leaving aside, for now, questions of fraud and mishap, what has taken place is a cashless transaction.

Money is regarded as so much information. Computers process information and pass it around between them with great efficiency. Therefore let computers handle the information which we call money. Money has been transformed, however, in such a process. Money, that is coinage, has traditional and symbolic significance. On the most mundane level it symbolizes a person's ability and choice to use his or her labour in exchange for a token. In replacing coinage by electronic 'money' the symbolism of the coin is lost. As Joseph Weizenbaum wrote in 'Technological Intoxication':

People once traded their labour directly for goods. Then money became an abstract quantification of human labour. Then cheques and other financial instruments became abstractions for money. Now we approach the so-called 'cashless' society in which electrons racing around computers and beyond any human being's ability to sense become abstractions for financial instruments. An observer from another planet will see people labouring in order to optimize the paths of electron streams flowing on their behalf in computers unseen and incomprehensible. (p. 305)

The fourth area of growing applications for microtechnology is that of *education* and education in its widest sense and at all levels. The most obvious invasion into education by the chip is seen in the rapid expansion of the market for pocket calculators and similar devices. These are essentially single chip systems and the range of product is now extensive. As well as conventional pocket calculators, which may contain scientific functions, may possess 'memory', or even be programmable, and which range from the very cheap to the fairly expensive in price, there are a variety of educational and novelty calculators. Typical of these are the calculators for learning to do arithmetic. The machine displays a sum, for example 23 + 14 and

waits for the answer. If you key in 37 the machine displays a
fresh problem. All four arithmetic processes are treated in this
way and the device can be used as a simple calculator as well.
Learning arithmetic then becomes a game and the child
develops the hacker syndrome.

A similar calculator does for spelling what the other machine
did for arithmetic. The novelty added here can be synthesized
speech: the machine 'talks' to you, asking you how to spell some
word or other. You key in the letters, which it reads out as you
go, and, if you get the correct answer, it praises you and gives
you another word. There are, of course, other variations
available on the calculator to enable a variety of spelling and
reading skills to be developed and there are several levels of
difficulty available. Perhaps of more interest to us is speech
synthesis, for nothing is pre-recorded on a tape as in a talking
doll.

When you speak into a microphone the sounds you make are
converted into a complex of electrical signals, which are
converted back into sounds in a loudspeaker. In recent years
computer scientists have been able to codify the signals that
represent speech and write computer programs that generate
those signals in their different combinations. In this way a
computer can synthesize speech by using a loudspeaker as its
output. Music can also be generated in this way and I know of
one program that gives a fair rendering of a Bach organ prelude
and fugue and sounds as if it were being played competently on
an electric organ. Speech synthesis is a highly complex
computation and yet it is now available on a relatively cheap
children's educational toy. When the machine 'says' 'SPELL
ONION', it is forming those words electronically and outputting the signals in a speaker. Such a toy provokes a strong
reaction from its user and creates a demand for its use out of
proportion to its abilities. Its educational value is arguable; at
present, however, its mid-Atlantic accent and dubious pronunciation are amusing and the 'talking' educational calculator is very much with us.

The computer in school, home or office has obvious educational functions but it seems to me that the most useful
educational function of a computer, of whatever size, is for
modelling dynamical properties of systems and for simulations.

Combined use of computational power and the imaginative application of computer graphics can result in the 'realistic' simulation of aircraft flight or the effect of pollution in a lake. An ecological problem can be analysed in terms of a number of interacting variables including the growth and reproduction rates of flora and fauna, the inter-dependence of those factors on annual cycles in the food chain, and so on; then the populations of an ecological system can be displayed graphically, simulating in a few seconds what in real life takes years. Similarly, the effect of fishing, or the introduction of a pollutant into the ecosystem, can be modelled, and this sort of simulation is instructive both in terms of the factors built into the program and its demonstrative ability. More sophisticated simulations such as that of aircraft flight will involve a large computer working in 'real time', that is functioning as things happen in the real world. As modern aircraft have computer controls for the wing and flying surfaces, for engine monitoring, navigation and instrumentation, all that is required for a complete simulation is to let the computer 'fly' the aircraft and respond to the trainee pilot at the controls. Of course, the craft is on land and not flying at all, but the computer can generate any or all of the problems a pilot might have to cope with. Suitable graphical output can even show other aircraft flying nearby in the view through the cockpit window. Crude versions of this sort of simulation are found as games in many amusement arcades but the real thing can be totally convincing.

Computers that 'teach' are also increasing in popularity and sophistication. Self-paced learning on a teaching machine enables students to work at their own speed, guided by the computer program in a question and answer session that moves on as the student learns. Such machines are used in science teaching, language learning and other technical subjects. Learning how to program a computer is a suitable subject for computer-programmed learning. A class of students with such machines can then all be learning different subjects at different points in a syllabus at the same time. The result is a change in educational procedures, the nature of taught knowledge and the role of the teacher. The invasion of the chip transforms all it touches.

It is worth commenting further on the transformation of

knowledge by computing technology as it is another example like that of electronic transfer of funds. Computers can manipulate any information that can be converted to binary digits; hence written words, mathematical expressions and so on can be 'computerized'. In education, textual material can be programmed into the teaching machine and it can be designed to be able to respond to questions by the student as well as prompt its own questions. However, knowledge does not just consist of words, phrases and expressions, but also inflexions, emphasis, presentation, body language and the whole area of tacit knowledge. None of that can be associated with the computer because it is a computer and not a human being. Whoever writes the program controls what is said, whereas all teachers are different and all are human. People learn not just by rote, memory and practice, but by human interaction, so knowledge embedded in a machine changes the nature of knowledge as traditionally presented, just as it changes money.

Finally I want to present some picture of the way that microprocessor applications affect us in the *home* and in our *leisure*. One example will suffice to show not only the way applications multiply, but also to demonstrate the power of the chip. Consider having a home central heating system controlled by a chip. The system will consist of a boiler, several radiators with control valves and a thermometer in each room. The thermometers, control valves and boiler controls will all be connected to the chip-based processor. Inputs will be a pre-selected program and temperature values, and the output will be heat from the radiators. Such a system can then be controlled dynamically. Each room can be heated to the extent required and its temperature profile can vary throughout the day. Furthermore, each room will be independent of the others in that you can raise and lower the heat in any room regardless of what is occurring elsewhere. In this way a house can be heated in the most efficient and most controllable fashion, quite differently from any conventional system. Again it is a matter of information, which can be manipulated according to the user's real requirements. The story does not end there, however, for the processor that controls the heating can do more.

Home security can also be controlled by the chip, simply by connecting up windows and doors to protection systems that are monitored by the processor. If anyone tries to break into the house the system sounds an alarm and, via the telephone, alerts the local police station automatically. I have linked the house processor to the telephone system surreptitiously and will extend that part of the system shortly. An additional bonus for home security involves connecting the lighting circuit to the chip so that, when the house is left empty for a while, it can appear 'lived in'. Lights can be turned on and off appropriately in the evening, simulating their normal use and suggesting to the outside observer that the house is being used. Naturally, the television and radio could also be switched on and off by remote control, the curtains drawn and so on, depending on how complicated you want to make the system. The house itself is transformed into an information system.

The use of smoke and fire detectors can then be linked through the silicon 'brain' in the house via the telephone to the emergency services, so adding safety insurance to the home as well as security. The telephone link will be sophisticated; a chip in the instrument will record the telephone numbers you use frequently eliminating the need to look them up. If a number is engaged it will try again for you until it receives an answer. If the home computer is linked to outside information services, including your bank, then telephone calls will be charged for automatically and you won't need to be sent a bill. This link to the outside world enables you, via your television screen, to have access to view-data systems, banking and even your local supermarket. Dialling the appropriate channel will show you prices for the day in the neighbourhood shops and you can order what you want, pay for it electronically and have the goods delivered later. Such systems are now in service both in the USA and the UK and indicate the shape of things to come.

Public services like retailing become transformed by the chip. The scanner used by the cashier reads the information encoded in stripes on the packets and tins and then displays and sums the prices of goods selected. It is also linked to the shop's storekeeping system and so 'knows' when the shelves need replenishing and when more goods need to be ordered from a depot, which itself will be largely automated. The public telephone uses a chip to add processing power to its service. Digital dialling and display enable you to pay for your call according to its exact length, displaying the current cost as you speak. You can pay by magnetic card, which is 'read' by the instrument and which deducts the cost from your credit as it does so. If you try to vandalize the phone it senses the attack and calls the police!

Many home gadgets, such as weighing machines, food processors, sewing machines and so on are increasingly made more versatile by chip control. Children's toys nowadays are frequently electronic and operated via stored programs. Games and other leisure activities are computer-oriented, including television games and computer-based chess. Incidentally many of the chess-playing systems nowadays can out-play most human chess players. Computer graphics and music synthesis enable 'painting' and 'composing' to become computer-based leisure pursuits. The list is endless.

The transforming power of silicon-based information process-ing turns the centre of the home away from the hearth and towards the television and its terminal. The processor runs the home and integrates the family into its circuits. Machines that 'think' remodel the world in electronic terms and the five areas covered in this chapter illustrate the extent to which that remodelling, that transforming power, is being applied. Where it might lead we now consider; that the world we know can remain immune to the changes brought about by this tech-nology is no longer possible. The invasion of the chip is a transforming force.

5 FUTURES

The future is inevitable; the form it takes is not. What eventually happens is never quite what is expected and yet speculating on future trends and predicting things yet to come are part of man's thought and culture. The future is shaped, at least to some extent, by the present, and forecasting, based on extensions of what obtains now, is the best that can be hoped for as far as prediction goes. What I present in this chapter takes the form of a discussion of what is being done now and being developed for future application, as well as some general consequences of the extension of the applications already accomplished.

Futures can be chosen, or at least it is possible to set out on paths to certain consequences. Choice for the future is limited to that because what lies ahead is unknown. People choose the path they hope will lead to where they wish to go. People with power choose to take the rest along paths that they think are suitable for them, for one reason or another, rightly or wrongly. The makers and promoters of technologies direct people along paths by presenting them with the technology. Once the technology is accepted at least implicitly, the choice is made and then who dares to stand in the path of technological progress? Technology is 'sold' as progressive and where technology goes society follows. We have to turn to ancient China or to early medieval Islamic science to find technologies set aside deliberately because they were incompatible with the aims those societies wanted to pursue. The Chinese discovered gunpowder but chose not to develop the gun. We in the West generally accept the notion of the technological imperative which, like natural selection and evolution, inevitably leads where it will and precludes purposeful change, directed progress.

The imperative implies that the invention of a new technique demands its adoption and development, and although there are countless examples of 'useless' inventions that no one wants and which are not developed but fade away, the general tendency has been to pursue possible developments for their own sake. The technological imperative concerns that self-motivated pursuit and implies that it is somehow inevitable. This approach to technology is, of course, questionable and involves broader considerations about society and man's relationship to nature, which is examined in more depth in Chapter 6. Nevertheless, technology is promoted and the future planned as if the idea of the imperative was true.

The technological imperative of computing and micro-electronics moves in a certain direction and presents us with various futures. Whether we shall be able to choose them or not remains to be seen. Whether they come into existence or not will not necessarily depend on our choice. That the potential for futures exists is not in doubt and several key developments arising now will shape those potential futures. It is to them that we now turn.

One of the research topics in computer development is the subject of 'artificial intelligence' or AI. This area of study is concerned with general-purpose, problem-solving programs that mimic human intelligence. Much of the work in AI is concerned with analysis of language and with 'learning' and the impetus of the work is to produce 'intelligent' machines. The long-term aims of 'artificial intelligence' are by no means in sight of being fulfilled and the difficulty of finding a suitable theory of semantics at present seems insurmountable. However, progress has been made in limited areas and for shorter-term aims. Robots have been developed by combining the technological skills of engineers and computer scientists with the software skills of the AI researchers while another major advance has been the production of machines that 'learn' and the development of 'expert systems'.

Machine learning consists of having a program, maybe consisting of a set of rules, which allows the machine to discover new rules or simplify or otherwise alter its rules in the light of its operation; that is by interacting with the world. A 'learning' program means that a machine can alter its instructions in the light of some intermediate result. An example of such a program was the system called BOXES developed by

Donald Michie at Edinburgh. BOXES consisted of a cart on a
track that was given the task of 'learning' how to balance a pole
by moving around rather like the way a hand has to move to
keep a pole upright. The system had a TV 'eye' and the program
consisted of rules about which way to move in order to achieve
the goal. However, the rules were imparted with randomly
scattered data so they were not necessarily correct rules. The
machine would have to find out how to balance the pole by
modifying the rules in the light of experience and even
combining and refining them to produce the optimum skill. As
the system gained 'experience' so it became an expert pole
balancer.

Programs can also 'learn by experience' by continually up-
dating their 'memory' as new information is given to them. So a
machine can be 'shown' an object, via its camera 'eye', and told
what the object is, for example a pencil. The machine analyses
the image in terms of its general shape and characteristic
features and can then attempt to distinguish correctly a pencil
from other objects. The more pencils it 'sees' the better it
becomes at identifying them because it 'learns' the essential
characteristics of the object partly by analysing the image it has
of the object but also by asking questions. It might, for instance,
enquire why an object was a pencil when it had not got a pointed
end, and could be told that pencils had to be sharpened to a
point. That information would be analysed and synthesized
with that already 'known'. In such a way a clear and
unequivocal description of the properties of pencils is built up
in the machine in the most economical way possible, with the
self-elimination of unnecessary facts; this is allied to an image-
processing capability, whereby visual pictures can be broken
down into unequivocal shapes, shades and surfaces to be
matched against the characterized and classified properties of
'known' objects.

Machine 'learning' by case history also takes place. Some
basic factors about a particular phenomenon, for example a
disease, are programmed into the computer together with other
fundamental data and some typical case histories that illustrate
the varying ways the disease has manifested itself through a
whole range of symptoms. The program analyses these case
histories and builds up its own picture of how the disease shows

itself. It is then presented with a range of cases to diagnose and its successes and failures indicated. It uses this information to modify its own picture of the disease and try again. By this method (the technicalities of which I shall not attempt to go into) the program 'learns' to diagnose one or more illnesses with a success rate that rapidly approaches 100 per cent. Machine 'learning', in the limited fashion so far demonstrated, is very efficient and effective.

Once machines can be programmed to 'learn' they can then be 'taught' to become 'experts'. The development of 'expert systems' is perhaps the most powerful use of 'artificial intelligence' research at the current time. An 'expert system' was defined by Donald Michie as 'a computing system which embodies organized knowledge concerning some specific area of human expertise *sufficient to be able to do duty as a skilful and cost effective consultant*' (*Micro electronics and Society*, ed. T. Jones, p. 115). A computer system developed with expert knowledge can act as a consultant in much the same way as present human consultants. When the development costs have been repaid the computer system then becomes cheaper than a human consultant, possibly more reliable, certainly not subject to the strains and stresses of human experts, and with the possible bonus of having been 'taught' by several experts. An 'expert system' could have within it all the expertise of several real human experts and therefore, in principle, be more of an expert than any one of them. Of course, such a proposition leaves aside all the tacit and other human aspects of knowledge but, that apart, one can see the logic of the case.

The 'expert system' may also be used to 'teach' in the sense of providing its expertise to people training in its subject. Already it has been reported that in one British teaching hospital, young medics not only prefer to be taught by computer but in practice learn faster and more accurately than their colleagues who learn from their human teachers. Expert systems have been set up in medical diagnosis, psychology, agricultural practice, chemical analysis, economics, geological studies for the mining industry, engineering and structural analysis, computer-assisted design as well as in mathematics and game playing. 'Expert librarians' or information systems are also high on the list of AI developments, because the notion of a really 'intelligent' system would include the ability to answer questions from one of many areas of knowledge. Certainly a computer-based information system that could pre-digest scientific abstracts would be an excellent consultative service for research scientists, provided it was sophisticated enough, and indeed the early stages of such a universal system have already been in operation for a few years.

One future that can be predicted with some confidence is that computer 'learning' and 'expert systems' will be developed at an increasing pace and spread over wide areas. It is quite conceivable that visits to the doctor will involve computer diagnosis as a routine; indeed the visit itself will become unnecessary as people with a home information system will be able to switch into the doctor's computer for diagnosis without the doctor's personal involvement, at least to begin with. The doctor's own role will then be quite transformed as he helps the computerized 'expert' by describing symptoms, authorizing medicines and acting far more as a nurse than as a doctor. He will be able to concentrate on offering comfort, sympathy and other characteristics of the caring professions, leaving the machine to work out the technicalities.

Similarly a visit to (or switching over to) a lawyer will mean consulting a 'legal expert system'. It has even been proposed that a computer could play the part of a judge, being capable of greater direct access to and more powerful analysis of past cases and legal precedents. Such a 'judge', it has been proposed, would give more reliable, more consistent and less biased judgements and present fairer summaries of trials to a jury than do human judges. It should be pointed out that such a system, although it would act impeccably over quantitative analysis of legal precedents and be capable of having access to vast stores of legal knowledge, could not match a human judge in the tacit judging of character of, for instance, accused or witnesses. Human response to humans, unreliable though it may be, biased though it may be, nevertheless is part of the human condition and no machine can parallel being a human. The machine is a tool and, however powerful or useful a tool, it must be kept as a tool not as a replacement for human interaction.

That said, many people prefer to be diagnosed by a machine, considering it more confidential, less judgemental, more objective than its human counterpart. Many would argue that judges should be replaced by an 'expert system' which would not contain the subjective quirkiness some judges display. The issue is still young and the debate over such future considerations will become more lively as the potential of these developments takes grip. The technologists will present the possibilities; society, they will argue, must choose, reject or modify these possibilities. The argument of the technological imperative holds that the inevitable will happen, that the realization of the potential is a 'must', not a choice. The technology has chosen itself. The market economists will argue that new developments will take over only if people want them, but their response will depend on what alternatives are available or are as readily available. At present 'expert systems' and machines that 'learn' are in existence. Their development is being continued for the future.

One aspect of 'artificial intelligence' already encountered is that of pattern recognition, which itself is a form of 'learning' and adopting given rules and conditions. So far, I have only mentioned recognition of patterns from visual data, carefully analysed; another major form of pattern recognition lies in sorting out those complex aural patterns we call speech. The intricacies of speech recognition involve not only problems of pronunciation, dialect, slang and rhythm but also the understanding of speech because of context, which brings the problem back to that of a lack of theory of language and semantics. These difficulties make speech recognition not just an exercise in technical application but an area of central theoretical interest and research. If this problem can be solved then many other difficult barriers to the achievement of high levels of machine 'intelligence' will also be overcome.

All this aside, limited progress has already been made with speech recognition programs. Some machines have been programmed to recognize a small vocabulary of words, spoken carefully or in one particular voice. There are machines that can 'listen' as well as 'talk back'. In the future there will be many more such programs and they will find many applications.

A machine that 'learns' can be taught to recognize a particular voice saying particular phrases and can use that knowledge for purposes of security and identification. When you go to drive your car, instead of using a key to unlock it, you will ask it to open the door for you. It may respond, like the sailors on HMS Pinafore, and say; 'If what?' To which you have to add, 'if you please'. By recognizing your voice as distinct from someone else's the car will unlock itself and a similar voice command will activate the ignition. If you have been drinking and your speech is slurred the car will not recognize your voice sufficiently and so won't let you drive it. The principle of verbal commands to machines is the core of this application and can be extended beyond the private car to aircraft control and for tasks where verbal commands enable a fast and 'no hands' alteration to be made.

A chip embedded in a plastic card, which can be used for credit validation and electronic funds transfer could also have a speech recognition part to it to prevent fraud and misuse. For the card to be validly activated you would have to speak to it, maybe giving your name and address or some pre-arranged code word. It could also have your thumb print encoded in its circuits so that if in doubt about your voice it could ask for your thumb print to be 'looked at' by an optical reader built into the terminal operating with such cards. Speech recognition will enable you to ask your telephone to dial you a number, your television to turn itself on or off, and so on; the possibilities are endless.

Speech recognition, like much research in artificial 'intelligence', is being developed by and for the military. Its purpose is twofold. There are fairly obvious military applications for verbal command of hardware or of verbal order-taking. You can imagine weapons that, if captured by the enemy, cannot be fired because they do not recognize either the voices or the accents. Such weapons could be programmed to self-destruct if tampered with. Then there is military (and civil) intelligence. Certainly this is the area where much research into optical pattern recognition has been developed, so much so that one US firm advertises itself to the public on the strength of the slogan: 'Teaching a "blind" computer to "see" a tank'. (At least they include the quotation marks!) Voice recognition would extend this to the ability to monitor the world from spy satellites and to listen in to telex and telephone calls. A computer 'trained' to listen for key words in conversations could monitor vast numbers of telephone calls, passing on 'useful' information, where it was found, to the relevant authority. Computers, after all, are very good at monotonous, routine work which surveillance certainly must be. The moral, social and legal problems involved by such possibilities will be looked at later; the future offered by such developments may make people feel safer or more insecure depending on their outlook but forecasts suggest that such schemes could be commercially viable by the end of the 1980s, and forecasts of developments in computer applications have been accurate in the last eight to ten years.

Artificial 'intelligence' has contributed a great deal to the development of robots. The word ROBOT conjures up all sorts of connotations exploited by science fiction writers and it originates from the Czech dramatist Karel Capek's play *Rossum's Universal Robots*, written in 1921. Robot comes from the Czech word meaning worker, in the sense of someone doing drudgery, and it implies mechanical men of some sophistication. Today robots are looked on much like computers are, as universal machines for doing practical work. Robots are not just automatic machines; they are fully automated and can be programmed to do a range of tasks.

Robots do not look like robots; that is they are not designed to appear as humanoids. Robots like C3P0 in *Star Wars* are purely science fiction, although it must be said that R2D2 does look very like the experimental robot developed at Johns Hopkins University in the early 1960s and called the Hopkins Beast, which was programmed to seek out electrical sockets so it could recharge its batteries. However, most robots look like boxes with mechanical arms and grippers for manipulating workpieces or they look like more ordinary machines, for example a fork lift truck, except that they do not have operators.

Robots consist of four main features: sensors, implementors, power supplies and computers. Typical sensors detect light, sound, pressure, distances and provide information to the computer of the position and operational status of all its mechanical parts and of its orientation in space and time with respect to its environment and work in hand. The implementors are the arms, hands, wheels and other manipulating devices with which the robot operates on the environment. The power supplies may be pneumatic, mechanical, electrical but more probably a combination of all three and the computer may be a medium-sized or large main-frame computer with direct, cable or radio link to the robot or it may be an internal microprocessor or both. Experimental work in robotics will be described in later chapters, our concern now is with their industrial application.

There are well over twenty thousand industrial robots in world-wide use at the time of writing, mostly to be found in Japan, USA and Europe. Their tasks range from simple transportation of boxes or parts around factory floors or warehouses to the building and assembly of cars. Robots are used for loading, sorting and packing boxes, metal working, soldering, brazing and welding. They are employed in glass works, inspecting and checking goods and in the assembly of parts of complex equipment. They are also used in maintenance and repair work, for example by testing electrical circuits and replacing faulty components. The example I present here, of how an industrial robot can be used and 'taught' to do a job, involves paint spraying.

Consider a robot with a flexible and highly manipulative extending arm, whose position and motion can be altered continuously and which, via complex sensing and feedback systems, 'knows' exactly where the arm is and how it is operating. The arm can be fitted with a paint spray nozzle, a tube to a source of paint, and controls to regulate paint flow. This 'paint sprayer' is now ready to work but needs instructions as to what to do. Spray-painting a complex object, like a tubular steel chair, requires some skill, so that paint is applied evenly over the whole three-dimensional surface. The chair may be suspended from a rotating arm, also a part of the robot, or at least linked to it and the chair, when painted, could be automatically passed to a drying room and another chair fetched from the production line. In order to instruct the robot sprayer, a human operator leads it through the process. The skilled sprayer takes the arm with the nozzle, which is fitted with a hand release to the paint spray and he proceeds to spray the chair. The arm merely records how it is being moved around as the sprayer does his work. Having been shown once, the robot can repeat the complex sequence of movements whenever required. It has 'learned' the human skill of spray-painting chairs.

As a general-purpose machine this robot could, just as simply, be 'taught' to spray any other object and could, with modification to its tools, be used for other industrial purposes. The transformation brought about by industrial automation leads to a removal of the emphasis on product as the machines can be programmed to make anything.

Robots are with us and their increased use in future is inevitable. As more are made their cost comes down and once their cost is equal to three years' salary of the worker whose job they will replace, then they become very economical to install. There is no reason, at such a price, why they should not pay for themselves within one to one and a half years, as they can work two or three shifts per day as required. At present some robots are matching that cost requirement. The more general-purpose the machines are the higher their cost, but even with more expensive robots their efficiency and work load capability make them a very tempting alternative to human labour for a manufacturer. New industries especially benefit from investing in robotic automation at the outset and so it is not surprising to find that robots are already building robots. In Japan an automated robot factory works day and night. During the day the human work-force checks the operation of the factory, but at night, after the people have all gone home, the factory work continues as if nothing had altered.

Computer-assisted design allows sophisticated design work to be accomplished largely by computer, eliminating much need for technical draughtsmen and other design workers. Robots, in that sense, are designing and building the next generation of robots. Use of computer-aided design and ergonomic assessment programs, like SAMMIE (System for Aiding Man–Machine Interaction Evaluation) and GRASP (Graphical Robot Assessment and Simulation Package), developed at the University of Nottingham, allows systems designers to evaluate how human or robot operators can best function in a work setting and modify the design of that setting accordingly.

For example, the size and position of rear-view mirrors on trucks and buses can be optimized with such design assistance by 3D simulation of the field of view from the driving cab. Alternatively the handling of a work-piece can be designed both in its positioning and in its sequential place in a series of manoeuvres by a production-line set of robot arms. This type of software greatly extends the range of the designer's capacity to try and test alternative options without the expensive business of building several prototypes.

The extension of these areas of applied research into the future has led to the concept of the so-called workless society, in which most manual, clerical and administrative work has been taken over by machines. With the development of 'expert systems' even professional work in such a society would become automated, leaving people with little or no work in any traditional sense. Such a view of society is also called the leisure society but that is a misleading term with propaganda overtones as it suggests that everyone will enjoy leisure activities rather than that they will be workless. A cartoon showed a worker sitting at the controls of a complex work simulator—the ultimate leisure pursuit!

Re-educating people to change the basis of their life and give up the so-called Protestant work ethic in favour of a leisure-based 'creative' life-style is one common response to this potential future; but the basis of the technology itself is interlinked with this work ethic and it may not be possible to have its fruits without its practice. Similarly the proposal to reintroduce handicrafts and cottage industries simply to counteract the boredom of a world where our material needs are provided by robots is naïve. The mental outlook of those who favour crafts is quite different from those who seek an automated society; the two attitudes are too dissimilar to be united in one societal model.

It is sometimes assumed that service industries will expand, and that personal service will be highly regarded, filling the work requirements of many people. However, service industries are being automated as quickly as manufacturing industries, or more so. Economic pressures in advanced industrialized countries are causing higher job losses in the caring and personal service section of the job market, so predictions based on present trends look gloomy. Service jobs will not, necessarily, fill the work gap in a workless society.

The picture, as it is painted, however, shows a rich, post-industrial society in which robots manufacture all the goods people want, creating wealth for society as a whole; at the same time people have a high standard of living, enjoying continuing education, hobby and leisure activities and developing human relationships, whilst having very little, if any, work to do. That is the image of the workless society and is the projection of where robotics leads. A part of that picture is the assumption, right or wrong, that people will, in fact, be re-educated for leisure, will be happy to play squash and go to the opera every day, if that is their wish, and neither expect nor want to work.

Other futures involve the *paperless* society and the *cashless society*. Both these potentials are aspects of an *information society*, or what James Martin called *the wired society*. These futures, which stem from present-day developments and so are not entirely fanciful, all involve world-wide networks of communications systems linking houses and businesses, government offices and leisure centres together in a giant web of information flow. Houses will become places of work and play, eliminating the need for costly transport, because you will be able to talk to your co-workers or friends, by video channel. The contents of documents will be transmitted from one place to another, eliminating paper mail and saving trees, as paper becomes obsolete. Contracts will be signed in two places at once, by using 'light pens' at a video terminal that produces a written document from a printer, if a hard copy is wanted. Money will become bits of information passed round electronically.

Two-way channels will enable TV terminals to serve as input as well as output devices. The viewer will be able to comment on and criticize the programme he is watching. Instant polls can be taken on issues, with viewers participating by sending their opinion over the lines to a vote-counting computer. Instant democracy could be extended to serious political decision-making.

Bank managers will be technicians and their ability to judge clients humanly and to take risks will be superseded by computers that sort out a person's credit status on hard, quantifiable data. The world will become enveloped in an electronic blanket: video, stereo, view data, networks.

The new technologies will reduce pollution because the techniques are 'cleaner' than the old mechanized industries. Congestion on the roads and even the spread of motorways will ease as people 'travel' by sitting at home, 'visiting' their friends by electronic communication. Disappearing paper means more trees, better ecological management, but at what price? Cultures will be eaten up as the satellite links spread to all the corners of the globe. It will be argued that those cultures that still remain distinct will merely be spread around the world by information networks, but in fact the 'wired society' is a product of one culture, an imperialistic culture, whose tools provide the means for global domination. Other cultures cannot be preserved within its encompassing network.

Technologies transform, and in these future worlds what transformations will have happened? A goods-dominated society will have become an information-oriented culture. There will be no cash, no paper, little work as we now know it. To read a newspaper will be to scan a TV screen, pushing buttons to flip the pages. To talk to an acquaintance will be to 'see' each other on screens, unable to touch, smell or taste things that otherwise could be shared; the meeting reduced to sight and sound and those not real, but sights and sounds emerging from electronic hardware. Shopping will be done by terminal, goods will be displayed on the customer's screen, selected and paid for automatically and delivered to the door. Exercise can be part of leisure. Factories will be run by robots, offices by computers. Children will be taught by machine; machines will act as doctors, lawyers and consultants. The home will become a new type of place, isolated from nature, defended against the have-nots.

There has been no mention in the literature, that I can find, of those who cannot and of those who choose not to participate in these futures. Some people, because of lack of education or lack of money, from handicap and inadequacy, will not get the opportunity to enjoy this world of information. If someone is not worthy, he will not get his card-with-a-chip and will not be able to pay by EFT. In a cashless society how do the have-nots pay? Already in the United States there are businesses which only accept credit cards; cash is not acceptable for it invites crime. If the have-nots have no access to the supermarket, no access to the fruits of the society, nor can they steal cash, where will they turn? Will the electronic home have to be fortified against those that play no part in the electronic life? Again, in the USA towns are being built and lived in, surrounded by patrolled walls to keep crime out, to protect the frightened haves against the have-nots.

What about those who choose not to participate, who refuse to have an EFT card, who *want* cash? What about those who want their children taught by people, who want to talk to people face to face, not image to image? What of those who choose not to have a home terminal, will they be able to shop, to discover the news, to vote? Will there be an alternative society parallel to the electronic one, a wired society and a wireless one? Are the futures, based on where this technology is leading, a form of progress, a cultural growing up or do they constitute the ingredients of a nightmare? Future outcomes are never what people expect and the two alternatives I have drawn are extremes. The wired society is being advocated strongly, being sought actively, its alternative seems to be neglected. The future will probably consist of ingredients from both possibilities but the concern now should be with the processes of choice.

The technological imperative demands the information society and demands it world-wide. It assumes that developments, such as those outlined here, constitute progress and social evolution to a higher form. Progress, however, implies some purpose, some goals to be achieved; rather than buy 'progress' for its own sake people should first decide what goals they seek and then choose how best to achieve those goals. The futures I have sketched in this chapter would all arise from where computing and communications technologies can take us. Whether those goals are what people want is not being determined nor seriously questioned, but neither are the consequences seriously examined. In order to assess this technology as it stands today and to evaluate where it might lead in the future requires a look at its past. It is in the light of the past, of past technologies and their place in changing society, and in the light of the origins of computing technology itself, that the new technology can be judged for its potential futures and for its effects on society and on individuals.

6 TECHNOLOGY AND MAN

The interaction of man with his technologies has transformed the world and has transformed man. The extension of man's natural senses and abilities, through the development of tools, techniques and the media of communication, has altered nature and man's attitude to it as well as reflected it. Incorporated into a technology is a segment of man's cosmology, his view of the universe, his own skills, reasoning and imagination. Built into each and every tool man makes, is an extension of man himself and yet the tool, the extension of man into his technology, reflects him imperfectly, distorts the image and operates on the world and on humanity in ways so different from those intended as to modify and modulate the world unexpectedly.

Combined with the power of technology to transform is its spell-binding power to fascinate. The psalmist's line, 'They that make them are like unto them', points out this power and Marshall McLuhan links it to the Narcissus myth. Narcissus as a word comes from the Greek *narcosis*, which also gives us the term narcotic, which means numbness. McLuhan, in *Understanding Media*, wrote:

> The youth Narcissus mistook his own reflection in the water for another person. This extension of himself by mirror numbed his perceptions until he became the servo-mechanism of his own extended or repeated image. The nymph Echo tried to win his love with fragments of his own speech, but in vain. He was numb. He had adapted to his extension of himself and had become a closed system. (p. 51)

This passage undoubtedly encapsulates much of the essence of technology. Narcissus' mirror symbolizes all technologies, reflecting man or some aspect of his capacities directly in an external form. We are used to thinking of technology in terms of heavy machinery, things with cogs and wheels, but silicon chip technology is not like that and the above myth illustrates the fact that even the surface of a pool, a natural phenomenon, can become a technology, an extension of man. Equally a technique, a process for doing something (maybe looking at one's own reflection), can become an external embodiment of human faculties and equivalent to technology, especially when seen as a thing in itself. This point, too, emerges from McLuhan's paragraph; the trouble with technology is not itself but our attitude to it, for we do not often recognize it for what it is, mistaking it for something that is an end in itself rather than a means to an end. Narcissus misunderstood the meaning of the image he saw in the water; it was a mirror, a means of seeing himself, and the reflection was not a 'real' object at all.

The numbness induced in Narcissus, which gives us his name, is also a general reaction induced by technology and by techniques. Travel by motor car numbs one's senses to the reality of the countryside, leaving the traveller exhausted and cut off, in other words numbed. Walking, on the other hand, unless pursued fanatically as a technique to be regarded as an end in itself, may leave the traveller physically tired but the senses, the sense of integration with the world, should be extended not numbed. Travelling on foot can be wholesome in a way that travelling by car (or train or plane) can never be; the technology drugs its user. Narcotic, apart from meaning numbness, also has the connotation of addiction and that, too, is true of technology. The car user uses the car instead of walking, even for journeys of only a few hundred yards. The technical means of 'easy' travel induces its use whenever possible not just when appropriate. The television viewer finds it difficult to switch off after one programme, but tends to see what is on next, just as the smoker has to have one more cigarette. People turn on electric lights because they are there even when natural light is in abundance. Technologies are not easy to switch off or leave aside, so the numbness they induce becomes reinforced.

Narcissus shows us the mythological picture of the hacker, fascinated with the system to the point of obsessiveness, to the exclusion of all else. The numbness induced by the technology reinforces this obsession for it blots out all other influences. The myth may seem to be an extreme case, as does that of the hacker, until we try to think of all the technologies we use in daily life and contemplate alternatives to each of them or the idea of not using any of them. Our own addiction to our extensions in technology is more than a pale shadow of that shown by Narcissus, and the reason for it is also given by McLuhan. He describes the 'addiction' in terms of the user of technology becoming a servo-mechanism of the technology, adapting to the technique and becoming thereby closed to the world. Man and technology are symbiotic, in that sense, because each feeds off the other; man invents the technology, develops an extension of himself and then adapts himself to the device of his own making. The servo-mechanism of such a cycle then prevents the user from returning to old ways because the mechanism of the new technique has excluded the thing it replaced. The feedback loop of the technology and its use can only be broken by willed effort. Such a procedure also manifests itself in the notion of the technological imperative: the idea that technology has a life of its own, what can be done must be done. It is the argument of a Narcissus treating his own reflection as an end in itself.

John Biram coined a term for man's obsession with technology and for the general misunderstanding that technologies and techniques are not ends but means to ends; the term is *teknosis*. In his book of the same name he argues that the teknotic attitude can be found in everyone and is related to so much of modern life that our whole culture suffers chronically from this 'disease of technical thinking'. Teknosis is an attitude of mind, part hacker syndrome, part Narcissus complex, whereby man worships idols of silver and gold and becomes like the objects of worship. Religious rituals, after all, are designed to help one reach upwards to God, so it is not surprising that the profane rituals of technique help one reach outwards towards one's own mirror image; a direction not likely to be helpful to one spiritually, as the goal is misplaced, or emotionally, as one's affections are directed to an image rather than to something 'real'. Teknosis implies unreality, which seems a strange notion when our technology, our hardware, seems so *real*, so predominant in all aspects of our physical environment. Teknosis is akin to Heidegger's notion of 'technicity', which W. J. Richardson has described thus: 'Rather it is the fundamental attitude in man by which all beings, even himself, become raw material for his pro-posing, contra-posing, (self)-imposing compartment with beings. Technology is simply the instrumentation of this attitude (p. 44).' The idea that technology is the 'hardware' by which man extends his attitudes, beliefs and thoughts is present in all the threads I have drawn together here from McLuhan, Biram and Heidegger. Technology reflects man and man is himself re-reflected by his technology.

This web of technical description and of technical implementation also redefines the world in its own terms. Marshall McLuhan has encapsulated this ability, indeed essential function, of all technologies in the phrase 'the medium is the message'. The transforming power of techniques is the technique not its content. Printing changed the medieval world dramatically in thought, practice and outlook, even though most people could not read, and not many even saw a book. Yet printing transformed the lives of most people in that society, because the medium of print, that new technology, changed attitudes, altered perspectives, redefined the world. It was the fact of print, not what was actually printed, that transformed society, and McLuhan is right when he comments that we too often ignore the medium and only see the content. The technology that, arguably, best illustrates his point is the contentless technology of electric light. The content is pure illumination and yet this medium, this technology, transforms man's individual life and revolutionizes society. All electric technology is pure information technology where the content is irrelevant. It is most starkly shown by the electric light but is demonstrated in computing and communications technology generally.

Electric light illuminates our physical surroundings. The information it provides comes from our relationship with that environment. If we are using the light to read a book then the book becomes the content of the medium of electric light. What the book is has no relevance to our altered perspective that the light has induced. The irrelevance of the content is shown more starkly when the light is turned on to brighten an already adequately lit corridor. Such usage of a technology also reflects our numbed reliance on it. How often do we stop to ask ourselves: 'Do I need to supplement the light in this room to see what I am doing now?'

One of the difficulties of discussing the irrelevance of content in assessing electric and communications technologies is that the information being communicated gets in the way. The effect of television as a technology is always masked by the programmes it has to offer. However, the programmes are irrelevant, the technology interacts with the viewer in many ways, irrespective of the content. The technology intervenes between person and commonly shared experiences. Discussing last night's TV programme with friends is more fulfilling than watching the programme in the first place. The important question is not what information you received but to what degree did the technology intervene between you and wholesome experience. In watching television with friends one finds that although each person is having identical images and sound presented to them, the experience violates each individual and does not bring them together into a common pool of shared human interaction. Electric media, operating on the central nervous system, engage people at deep levels of attention, narrowing down the focus of their senses, enmeshing them in contentious webs.

Although the printing press is often regarded as the turning point of medieval society, Lewis Mumford, in *Technics and Civilization*, suggests that the earlier invention of the clock was more crucial as an agent of change. The mechanical clock introduced a linear, progressive, sequential awareness of time, in place of the organic, cyclic perception of time man had before. The clock transformed society and subjected people to the rule of time, to work by the clock, to do things when the church clock struck the hour or quarters, rather than when ready to be done. As I have said in my own book, *On Time*, the mechanization of time, its subjugation to technology, paved the way for the mechanization of speech, through the printing press, and the mechanization of space through modern transport. However, the mechanical clock, as Weizenbaum so rightly pointed out, also introduced another aspect to technology, namely autonomy.

Most technologies extend human faculties. The wheel extends the foot, the telescope extends the eye, our clothes extend our skin. Such technologies, extensions of the human body, can be classed as *prosthetic*, artificial 'limbs and organs'. The clock, however, does not extend a human faculty, despite the fact that our bodies react to several internal biological 'clocks'. The clock is an *autonomous* machine, automatic in that it works by itself unaided, once wound up, and independent of man for what it does. The clock embodies a model of planetary motion to provide elements of time, it does not reflect man physically at all, neither does it measure a physical quality, for time is immaterial, but it does reflect man's ideas. The transforming power of the clock lies in its autonomy, its independence of man. It is a mirror of a rational idea.

Lewis Mumford wrote that the clock 'disassociated time from human events and helped create the belief in an independent world of mathematically measurable sequences', to which Weizenbaum adds: 'the clock created literally a new reality . . . that was and remains an impoverished version of the old one'. The disassociation, the abstraction of time from human experience, is the consequence of the autonomy of the clock. The medium is bereft of human qualities, independent from nature, and so the message, too, is abstract, objective. It is this objectivity also that impoverishes man's life by placing a framework around society that removes people from their previous more intimate relationship with nature. The grid of time set up mechanically is a harness that reduces the richness of life. That is how all technologies work in one way or another and the inevitable impoverishment they cause must be weighed against the material advantages that their acceptance implies. That impoverishment, that removal from nature, arises with all technology but seems most powerful and embracing with the autonomous clock. The extensions of man, being of man, have more subjectivity than does the abstract machine.

If the clock was the first autonomous machine then the second one is the computer. The computer is not prosthetic, it is not an extension of the brain, and, despite Marshall McLuhan's analysis, I do not think that the computer and its extension through electronic communications technology is essentially an extension of the central nervous system. This latter analogy seems plausible but it does imply the brain/computer equation which I do not think is appropriate, although the electric technologies do act on the central nervous system. Rather than extend man's own characteristics, the computer, like the clock, encapsulates an abstract notion, it embodies one of man's ideas. The computer models the notion of pure rationality, man's ideal view of his own intelligence. The impoverishment comes from the limitation of that view of man, for intelligence is far more than pure rationality. The power of the computer, like the power of the clock, comes from its independence of man, leaving man, with his Narcissus-like infatuation with his own created images, to redefine himself in the image of the computer.

Technologies embody man's view of the world and his relationship with it and hence the machines man builds are symbols of man's re-created world. As symbols are a means of communication so all machines are communications media and their form is their pervasive message. The anonymity of a computer, its facelessness, symbolizes man's own loss of face and faith, his own anonymity in a world of machines, a world become teknotic. The network of mechanical time laid down by the clock has been hardened and overlaid by a network of information channels. The clock changed man from being a creature in nature to being a master of nature. Electronic microtechnology is changing man from being master of nature to becoming slave to the autonomous machine. The invisible web of information, the interfaced black boxes, act as agents for change, as do all technologies, but, whereas prosthetic tools embody the designs of their own replacement, the autonomous computer embodies man's own replacement by the machine that 'thinks'.

Another way in which the relationship between man and machine can be understood is by examining the relationship between science and technology and their historical development. Such an account will be helpful both with regard to assessing the place of technology in society and appreciating the background out of which computer technology has emerged. The account presented here is of necessity condensed but fuller versions can be found elsewhere both in standard histories or in analyses such as that by Jaques Ellul. My own analysis is much closer in spirit to the latter in that I place technology before science in its historical and developmental importance, although I shall argue that science and technology cannot really be separated from each other nor from the society in which they exist.

There are many definitions of science, but most include the idea that science is distinguished as being concerned with the understanding of nature, and that technology, or applied science, is concerned with its control. Of course, these two parts of pure and applied research are inextricably intertwined, for to be able to control requires some understanding and understanding for control requires a special method. A more critical argument about science says that its understanding of nature is developed in order to control, rather than just to understand. The application of knowledge, which is so often considered secondary to its discovery, may well be the driving force behind the discoveries made using the scientific method. The historical account I present here stresses this view, that modern scientific knowledge pre-eminently stems from a desire for application.

The notion of 'science for its own sake', the idea that knowledge should be pursued just because it is intrinsically interesting, is a modern idea, although it has its roots in classical Greece. The science and technologies of past cultures tend to be viewed with that thought in mind, but it is an inappropriate perspective. Ancient and traditional science is not the same thing as modern science. Although 'science' means knowledge, the term was not confined to meaning either empirical knowledge or to quantifiable knowledge. Science was not even restricted to meaning knowledge of the physical world and certainly traditional sciences included such areas of thought as astrology and alchemy as well as metallurgy and medicine. Past cultures were God-oriented and the thought, and hence the sciences, much occupied with sacred mysteries. Mathematics, then, was a science of number yet more akin to what would now be termed numerology. The mystery of numbers, their qualities, were more important than their quantitative manipulation. So, for example, the number π (the ratio of the circumference to the diameter of a circle) was not treated as a useful constant in geometric calculations, but was regarded as a sacred quantity whose value, as far as it could be known, was held secret by the priesthood. Such an idea appears quaint and even superstitious to people today, but that is because the present age is quite unfamiliar with sacred thought. Modern western culture is a secular culture and judges religious cultures from that position.

Looking back at ancient Babylon we see a science of planetary positions. In ancient China the royal observatories kept records that span two thousand years, the longest sequence of scientific observations in the history of mankind. The Chinese recorded planetary motions, the appearance of comets, the aurora borealis and even sunspots, in addition to atmospheric and meteorological phenomena. Viewed from our perspective this looks like evidence for a science in the modern sense, just as Japanese sword-making looks like modern metallurgy. However the Babylonian and Chinese observations were not concerned with trying to discover the nature of the stars and plants, as is modern astronomy, rather the observations were entirely practical, applied knowledge sought for astrological ends. Divination and prediction were the sciences being practised and were used both for mundane purposes, making political, economic and legal decisions, and for religious ends, to understand the mysteries of God. What appears like an ancient pure science is in fact a very practical applied one.

Ancient Greece seems to be the place where a technology-free science developed, and certainly the forerunners of Newton and Einstein can be traced in people like Hipparchus and Democritus. Perhaps more typical, although the point is arguable, was Pythagoras and his school, who treated mathematics and geometry as mystical systems. The Greeks do not seem to have developed a technology except in their architecture, which brought together the science and art of the day in a practical expression, the building of temples: again a religious context, and very similar in expression to that of medieval Europe. In contrast, however, the Romans, whose civilization was motivated by power and imperialism, were great technologists. There was no Roman science, all knowledge developed was entirely practical because imperialism necessitates a great deal of technology. To maintain an empire a complex infrastructure has to be constructed and the Romans developed technologies, mostly in what would nowadays be called civil engineering, to maintain that infrastructure. In contrast to the Greeks, who disdained practicalities and had to import essential techniques from the Middle East, the Romans disdained pure intellectuality and governed a vast empire by the application of technique and technology.

What appears like science, in terms of interest in phenomena for their own sake, is rarely found in cultures other than our own, but the ancient sciences were practically oriented and served the religions of those people. Science and technology were seen as means to an end and not as ends in themselves, which is the teknotic form of the relationship between man and technique, although the Romans displayed a teknotic attitude and possibly the Egyptians too. Knowledge and its practical implementation are inextricably interwoven in every case and are expressed through the underlying direction of the societies in which they appear. The metaphysic of the society directs the path along which knowledge is sought and applied. This is clearly seen in other cultures but is just as true of our own society and of our own time. Although it is often thought that science follows wherever knowledge leads, such a thought is but another expression of the technological imperative. That science *must* pursue its own ends is nothing more than propaganda and evidence from history shows it has never worked that way. In other cultures, as was true in the fairly recent past of Western society, knowledge and its pursuit was bounded by the principles of belief the society held. The same is still true today even if the imperative is part of the expression of today's beliefs and the boundaries seen in other cultures and times have mostly been eliminated in modern Western society.

In the seventeenth century in western and northern Europe something happened which changed the established pattern of man's thought. For about three hundred years a series of changes, such as the development of the clock and of printing, prepared the way for a radical change in perspective that has transformed the world. In the seventeenth century modern science emerged, born from the work of Copernicus and Galileo and brought to fruition by Newton. Yet modern science was only a manifestation of that change and not the change itself. The emergence of humanism in the Renaissance, the exploration of the world by Columbus, Magellan and da Gama, these too are signs of the change. The decline of magic, the rise of Protestantism, the replacement of feudalism by a capitalist economy, all occurred at this time; for man's relationship with nature and his attitude to religion altered his whole perspective on the universe. From the fourteenth century onward reasoning began to put more emphasis on a materialistic attitude and less on a spiritual. Exploration of the physical planet replaced inner journeys. The rise of banking emphasized the role of money as something distinct from what it symbolized. There was a change in world view from an organic, cyclic, ritualistic life, to one that became increasingly linear, progressive, manipulative. Man stepped out of nature, in western Europe, and set aside the symbolic view of the world that remained in other cultures. It was this change, from sacred to profane, that came about most distinctly in the seventeenth century and which gave rise to modern technology.

The world viewed as an object rather than as a symbol led directly to the perception that man could directly manipulate the natural world, hence Bacon's dictum that 'knowledge is power'. Of course, Bacon was referring to the new knowledge, the scientific potential, and he fully realized the danger of following such a path. The new knowledge, although disguised as knowledge for its own sake, was essentially knowledge for manipulation, which implies a new technology. Professor Acquaviva wrote in his book *The Decline of the Sacred in Industrial Society* this passage: 'in the writings of da Vinci, Bacon and others, the outlook of the new world of the machine was already implicit. There was a desire to break the net of symbolism that seemed to keep man at a distance from the real nature of things (p. 106).' The symbolic and sacred attitude contrasted starkly with the possibility of regarding nature as object and of taking it literally, and it is this literalness that characterizes the age.

Allegorical knowledge is not 'useful' in the sense of being manipulative but the transfer from an allegorical cosmology to a literal one enabled physical phenomena to be used; not in the way nature had always been used, by working with and in it, but used in the sense of exploited, nature as a set of objects was there to be conquered. By Newton's time the literal approach was fully established, not only in the new science but also in religion. The Protestant revolution that had swept northern Europe was also literal in approach, regarding the Bible as a source of direct truths. Newton prided himself on his ability to give a literal translation of any biblical passage and his interest in establishing a biblical chronology overrode his interest in physical phenomena. The link between the origins of science and the rise of Protestantism has been described by many authors and both phenomena share a literal stance, a material-istic philosophy.

The change from a symbolic perspective to an objective one also gave rise to a new attitude to authority and tradition. Luther and the Protestant reformers challenged the authority of Rome, scientists challenged the authority of all traditions over any teachings about nature. The motto adopted by the Royal Society, when it was founded in 1662, was *Nullius in Verba*: 'we take no man's word for anything'. The notion of the spirit of free enquiry that lies at the root of modern science and most modern thought stands out in contrast to all traditional cultures, whose basis is a tradition, a metaphysic, beyond dispute. Free enquiry also implies being free to pursue whatever one likes and hence to exploit nature and one's fellow men if that leads to power, riches or even personal fulfilment. The profit motive as well as rationalization both originate from this transformation of world view.

Whether modern technology stemmed from this change in attitude or caused it is arguable and unresolvable. Certainly technology played a more central role than is generally acknowledged. The machine objectifies and abstracts. The clock mechanized time and print mechanized speech. The particular way by which nature came to be read literally was the same as that by which already, in the seventeenth century, machines had been designed; that is by reducing the essence of a phenomenon to pure quantity. Literal thinking is quantitative thinking, with no place for the poetic, the allegorical and the purely qualitative. The French sociologist, G. Simondon, wrote:

By reducing the object to nothing but its dimensions, technology does not recognize in it any internal or symbolic meaning or any significance beyond its purely functional utility ... the object is sufficient in itself and is not the carrier of intentions. For this reason, one might say that 'technology desacralizes the world' to the extent that it progressively imprisons man in nothing but objects without allowing him to catch a glimpse of a higher reality. (Acquaviva, p. 140)

In this passage the quantitative theme links the turning away from the symbolic to a decline in religiosity. The abstraction of the world in literalness, creating the notion of the neutrality of objects, acts as a force for secularization. Certainly the scientific age has been accompanied by a decline in religion but, as it stems from an irreligious view of the world, that consequence is not surprising.

The centrality of technology, at least in accelerating the rise of modern science, can be exemplified in all the 'new sciences'. Galileo revolutionized astronomy by using a telescope, a new technology and one that came from northern Europe, and he altered the path of physics by developing the pendulum and other techniques for careful measurement of phenomena. Modern astronomy, conceived with a new instrument, was launched in England by the establishment of a Royal Observatory and an Astronomer Royal. The intention was not to understand the heavens, however, but to find a reliable method for determining longitude. The aim was practical, to provide a navigational service, and it was such amateurs as William Herschel, who later found 'pure' interest in the nature of heavenly bodies.

As navigation provided the motive for astronomy, so mining techniques led to the science of geology. New farming technology gave rise to agricultural science and the development of the steam engine led to the theoretical study of thermodynamics. In every case science stems from technology but then gives rise to new applications and new technologies. A loop becomes established with 'use' as its driving force. King Charles II, who founded the Royal Society, was 'graciously pleased' with the efforts at measuring longitude at sea, but he found the fundamental research into measuring the weight of air nothing more than a 'childish diversion'.

The industrial revolution was a technological revolution not a scientific one. The technologists were practical men, farmers, mill owners, engineers. The 'soulless' machine replaced human craft and modified the tools of traditional crafts, with their own symbolism and ritual practice, into the objects of mass production. The conquering of nature also meant the conquering of the work-force. The machine replaced muscle power and the labourer became slave to the machine. Nature was desacralized and man was dehumanized by the rapid growth of technological industry, the development of factories, pollution, slums, the movement away from the land into the growing cities, with wealth for some but poverty for many. The machine engineered the work-force, management separated planning from production, knowledge from skill, and where possible skill was replaced by mechanization. As David Landes wrote, in *The Unbound Prometheus*: 'Substituting machines for human skill and inanimate power for human and animal force ... brings about a shift from handicraft to manufacture and, so doing, gives birth to a modern economy' (p. 1).

In the nineteenth century it was recognized, at least in part, that science was becoming more useful in improving technology. The loop of technology/pure science/applied science was turning full circle and technology was being improved by the labours of science. The setting, however, was industrial technology where improvement invariably meant enabling the machine the better to emulate human skill, to produce more and to produce more efficiently and economically. Better machines maximize profit for the machine owner. Nevertheless, even by the end of the Victorian era there were still rather few professional scientists, mostly to be found in universities and such places as the Royal Institution in London. Many scientists were amateurs, clergy, monks, gentry and the single factor that changed that position was war.

Hilary and Steven Rose call the two World Wars the Chemists' war and the Physicists' war. The 1914–18 war was dominated by the chemical industry and its research efforts into explosives and poison gases, backed by the metal, glass and dyestuffs industries. Germany was quicker to exploit its own chemical industry and to realize the importance of science in producing weapons; the lesson was eventually learned by the British, but not before many of its young scientists, alongside the youth of the whole nation, had been used as cannon fodder and killed. Nevertheless the First World War professionalized science and demonstrated that scientists had a part to play in leading technological innovation.

The Second World War was predominantly a physicists' war. Radar, electronics and, of course, the development of the atomic bomb, were amongst the contributions science made towards the easy relationship that linked science to the military. Among the products of that alliance was the computer but it was the bomb that illustrated horrifically the lost innocence of science. With Hiroshima and Nagasaki science came of age and the primacy of science as the leading edge in man's attempted domination of nature, begun about three hundred years before, was established.

Since 1945 the dominance of science has been essentially unchallenged and has permeated the whole world. Governments pour money into science and technological research, mostly through defence departments, and science and its products have transformed life in much the same way that industrialization changed eighteenth- and nineteenth-century England. The spread of communications and world-wide military technology has altered man's relationship with nature, removed mankind even further away from that sense of being 'in nature', and has emphasized the idea that man can create his own environment. Space research, conquering the moon and developing space laboratories, is an advanced expression of man's desire, and ability through technology, to dominate his environment.

Two points emerge from this brief history. First, that the transforming power of technology has been the essential ingredient in the development of science, rather than vice versa. The application of knowledge has determined what knowledge is to be sought and the realization, by Bacon for example, that the sort of knowledge we call modern and scientific, is sought *in order to* 'effect all things possible'. The second is that technology and science is also shaped by the society in which it is found; that science and technology have a large social and political component to their direction and guiding philosophy. The spread of modern science and technology reflects and is a manifestation of the 'successful' secular imperialism of European and North American society.

An implication that arises from this historical approach is that technology (and science) in the last three hundred years or so are somehow different or distinct from previous technologies. To some extent I think this is true, and to see why and how the difference arises requires an analysis of two approaches to technique. These two types of technology I shall refer to as sacred and secular. Sacred technology can be distinguished as being a means for expressing a religious feeling and being used to religious ends—maybe the glory and worship of God.

There are two main expressions of such a sacred technology. The first of these can be referred to as the craft tools. Handmade from simple materials, wrought by skill and ingenuity, these tools were usually made by the owner and user of the tool, although specialization into wheelwright, blacksmith and so on occurs. Craft tools are essentially prosthetic, extensions of the hand and foot, enabling the crafts of agriculture and building, cookery, pottery and weaving to be pursued. These tools are central to the rituals of the crafts, and contain special symbolic significance. The vestiges of such technologies today are to be found in violins and other musical instruments, but in Western culture most such tools are to be found either in museums or replaced by modern counterparts, although some do still exist. The craft tools are sacred technology expressed through the mundane tasks of life.

The second form of sacred technology is that which is developed especially for religious ends. The Greek temples were masterpieces, not only of building technique, but also of architectural design. Medieval cathedrals remain as breathtaking examples of the skill and ingenuity of their master builders. Iconographic art and Gregorian plainsong are artistic techniques directed to the glory of God, and similar examples are to be found in all religious societies throughout the world. The American Indian's totem pole, Balinese dances, Hindu statuary and Shinto temples are religious expressions made manifest through technology and technique. In most traditional cultures this religious technology is the high point of development whilst the craft tools provide the day-to-day needs.

Secular technology, on the other hand, does not recognize gods other than efficiency, progress and possibly profit and power. However, efficiency and progress are not ends in themselves but means to ends that are not specified. Progress towards what ideal; what effect is being sought? Secular technology is an end in itself and therefore becomes imperialistic, obliterating and trivializing other forms of technology and even its own earlier products. The Roman Empire abounded with developments in military and civil engineering, while craft tools were frequently degraded to the status of the slaves who used them. Religious art and architecture declined through repetition and reproduction, whilst the new architecture was developed via the aqueduct and Colosseum. The parallels with modern technology need little emphasis, except to comment that our technology is primarily military and its spread to all parts of the globe is nothing if not imperialistic. Instead of circuses we have television as the mass entertainment and slaves have been replaced by the labour-saving gadgets. Secular technology is technology dedicated to making money and gaining power and the spread of modern industrial products— cars, aircraft, electronics goods and weaponry—have led to concentrations of power and the accumulation of great wealth by a few at the expense of the masses. The populations of the developed countries may be affluent by world standards but the rich are richer yet again. Secular technology is a power-concentrating technology and the idea that the devices and machines produced by such technology are somehow neutral, are simply objects which carry no intentions, is a falsehood.

Technologies, all technologies, stem from a social, economic, political, religious and cultural setting. Tools are man's expression of some aspect of his needs, his wants, his hopes and aspirations. The extensions of man, like man himself, are not 'merely objects' but contain a subjectivity that has shaped them as they are. The notion of objectivity arises from the abstraction of reality that the clock epitomized for time and that the computer does for thought; yet time and thought are not 'neutral' objects, independent of quality, or of their perception. Seeing tools as neutral things is to regard their usage, their 'content' in McLuhan's terminology, as the important factor and to ignore the essence of the things themselves; the medium itself has a message, it carries its inbuilt intentions.

For example, consider an electric, automatic washing machine. Such a piece of machinery may appear value-free, neutral to most people in Western culture, merely because it is so commonplace an object. However, if such a tool was handed to an Australian aborigine, or a bushman in the Kalahari, it would be little more than a useless piece of metal. In practice, the outer casing might come in handy but most of it would be junk. Why? Because built into the washing machine are the intentions of its makers and the cultural values of the society that produced it. To someone of another culture, whose motivations are quite different, the object has no use. The washing machine comes with the values built into it of a modern, industrial, consumer-oriented society. The machine requires electricity, piped water and drainage services. It is dependent on a detergent industry and systems of transport and money exchange, specific to its cultural background. It has also been produced with a certain attitude to work built into it. It is not neutral at all; to accept a washing machine is to accept a specific way of life, a specific attitude to nature, a specific attitude to man's place in the world. The technology is highly value laden. Its non-neutrality applies, of course, not just to the bushman but also to ourselves.

The arguments about the neutrality of science and technology seem to me to be propaganda urging acceptance for technicity, for adopting the 'faith' of science. Max Black has suggested it is an argument to cover up the moral irresponsibility of most scientists and technologists. Certainly, accepting the proposition that science and technology are neutral, are objective and independent of any particular stance or metaphysical attitude, means accepting the technological imperative, accepting the argument that research leads wherever it leads and that the paths opened up must be followed.

Accepting science's neutrality also allows its practitioners to work on problems that are 'technically sweet', such as the development of the hydrogen bomb, regardless of the nature and impact of the end product. Neutrality then becomes a defence, just as the inevitability of following where science leads is a defence, to doing what is interesting to the technician; again the means becomes an end in itself.

It seems to me that the neutrality argument is quite false, as both science and technology are demonstrably value laden. The scientific method itself springs from an attitude to the world and hence is imbued with that attitude. The work of scientists and technologists is performed within a social structure and a particular scientific setting. Research is directed by this intellectual environment, which itself is influenced by economic, social and political factors. The questions asked and the way answers might be formulated are culturally determined, so the issue of neutrality becomes a form of modern superstition, an argument to allow 'progress' to be made in the areas of science and technology, for means to become an end in themselves.

The non-neutrality of technology is expressed partially in its goals, in where its development leads; so the futures already discussed, the ones that microtechnology may lead to, are themselves imbued with the goals of the society that has produced such a technology: indeed the technology has been made to achieve those goals. The non-neutrality of machines implies that 'progress' is defined in terms of particular cultural values and is not an independent, objective thing in itself. However, the notion of progress is frequently put over as if it were culture-free, just as is the argument about neutrality. The future should therefore be one of choice, but the choice should be presented in terms of social factors, not in terms of machines. Technology should be a means to an end, not an end in itself. Allowing the technology to determine the end is to prejudge what that end is. Rather a choice of ends should be debated and the appropriate technology found for the chosen end. To disguise this issue in terms such as 'neutrality' and 'progress' is to confuse the real nature of technology and of the issue in question.

Technology and man are locked together on an international scale, each dependent on the other. Where modern technology comes from I have attempted to show; to a study of how computing technology continues that history, we now turn. The fact that communications and information technology is the current area of rapid development should be set against the background of man's relationship with his tools and their impact on human life and thought. However close we are to the latest device and developments we should not be blinded to the fact that we are looking at mirrors and we may become, like Narcissus, beguiled by what we see.

7 THE ORIGINS OF MICROTECHNOLOGY

The history of modern technology can be regarded as a gradual, though accelerating, transition from the sacred to the secular. There is more than just a close correlation between the decline in religiosity and the growth of industrial societies, for, in my view, the latter grew from an essentially irreligious, secular view of nature. However, there is another, parallel, way of viewing this change, and one that I think is especially helpful in locating the origins of present-day computing and micro-technology: that is to view the transition as a movement from quality to quantity.

The continual abstraction of the world, advanced by the scientific method and its manifestation in technology, is achieved primarily by reducing things to numbers. René Guénon has written in *The Reign of Quantity*: 'the chief characteristic of (the scientific) point of view is that it seeks to bring everything down to quantity, anything that cannot be so treated is not taken into account, and is regarded as more or less non-existent' (p. 85). This tendency can be discerned through-out the history of science and its effects can be seen in the transforming power of technologies. By abstracting a general characteristic of phenomena and concentrating that abstrac-tion, not only can powerful instructions be written for manipu-lating some aspect of the world, but also an apparently deep insight can be gained into the nature of things. The proof of validity for the insights or 'laws of nature' is that they can be used and they do work.

Just as technologies create dependencies so do scientific theories. By reducing complex phenomena to their quantitative aspects, laws of nature can be extracted which mirror the quantitative observations or facts. The success of predictions made by using these laws then justifies the exclusion of anything non-quantitative in their format. This leads to the view that the qualitative is 'useless' and somehow not 'real'.

Hence a philosophy that was only implicit becomes strongly explicit and takes the form of scientific reductionism.

Science works by limiting a phenomenon to its key ingredients. For example in examining motion the ingredients examined are the mass of moving objects, their position and their velocity (how they change position with time). It is deemed unnecessary to include any other factors in analysing motion. The field is restricted to those factors which are themselves quantified both analytically (through algebra and geometry) and numerically. Hence science works by reducing phenomena to certain key factors which will have specific and orderly interrelationships. In order to explain the complex, things are reduced to their components, and only to those components that are essential to a quantification that leads to control and use. For example the colour of moving objects could be quantified but colour is not a necessary factor in determining how to control motion.

Modern science is essentially reductionist in philosophy because *all* its techniques seek to reduce to pure number, and factors essential for use; the term 'descriptive' or 'qualitative' is almost always used in a derogatory sense. Yet a descriptive science, as E. F. Schumacher has pointed out, is a rich and complex potential form for science, in which the qualitative, the individualistic and particular are not sacrificed on the altar of quantity, uniformity and the statistical. In a descriptive science colour would also be described because, though it is not essential for control, it is a part of the phenomenon being described.

The quantitative scientific method developed with Galileo, Kepler and Newton; they encapsulated general properties of motion into specific scientific laws, which are, in effect, recipes or sets of instructions for doing things. Newton's Second Law of Motion, for example, expressed as $F = ma$, means that a force, F, will be required if you want to accelerate (a) a particular mass (m). This instruction is quite general or universal and is seen therefore as a law of nature; it is in practice only an instruction based on quantifying the way masses are moved by applied forces.

I have described the transition from a study of quality to that of quantity as also being a change from sacred to secular in outlook. It will be observed that scientists, like Newton, who played key roles in this transition, were not only religious but also saw God's handwork in the mathematical beauty they were discovering. There is no conflict here between the secularizing effect of the scientific method and the move away from a sacred view of nature. Because the specific, instruction-writing, method of science is so effective in use and application, because scientific knowledge is power, as Bacon prophesied, the qualitative has declined. The non-essential factors of phenomena have not just been left out, they have been neglected, forgotten and, at the extreme, denied. Such an attitude is allied to a non-religious outlook because not only is some of God's handiwork being ignored, but also those parts that are ignored, the individual characteristics of things, are frequently the things that mean most to people. So, although the turn to quantity began with God in mind, God was easily set aside as being another non-essential factor, and forgotten along with the other 'qualitative' factors.

By the nineteenth century, following the development of steam engines, pumps, and some fundamental chemistry and physics, scientific laws became statistical, further reducing phenomena to pure number. By treating things as members of large groups, some general properties of those things can be extracted by looking at the behaviour of the whole group. That is the basis of statistical description, although it must be pointed out that no single member of the group may actually exhibit the general characteristic that emerges. For example, the average age of a group of people might be 48 years and 3 months, although no one in the group is of that age. Statistical laws work well, just as do other 'laws of nature', but such 'laws' are also abstractions made under certain assumptions and only using certain chosen factors. For example, it is assumed that all atoms or molecules of a particular gas are identical, that repeatable events are similar, despite the fact that they occur at different times and places, and so on. Such assumptions may be perfectly reasonable and the fact that statistical laws 'work' justifies their adoption, but nevertheless statistics consist of highly quantified and abstracted properties of things.

The advance of science can be traced as the advance of an increase in quantitative reductionism. Einstein's theories of

relativity, especially the General Theory, reduced vast ranges
of phenomena to simple mathematical equations (well, at least
simple equations in essence, even if they turn out to be rather
complicated to understand). The development of quantum
theory in the first thirty years of this century, however,
advanced reductionism considerably and paved the intellectual
way for computer technology. Quantum physics has two
interesting aspects to it that are relevant to this discussion,
firstly that its laws are statistical, not at a macroscopic, large-
scale level, as were those descriptions of nineteenth-century
physics, which dealt with large populations of particles, but at
the sub-atomic level. Quantum physicists claim the primacy of
statistical quantification as the basis of physical reality.
Secondly quantum physics, as its name implies, deals with
quanta, plain numbers of things. The premiss on which
quantum laws are based is that all physical phenomena can be
reduced to discrete units that can be counted, hence everything
is reduced to pure quantity.

   There are physicists, David Bohm for example, who find this
reduction to quantity unsatisfactory, and the assumption that
quantum physics is the ultimate scientific theory nothing more
than a modern myth. However, the current standard picture
(presented for example in Peter Atkin's book *The Creation*) is
that all biology (including sociology and psychology) can be
reduced to chemistry, which itself is reducible to physics and all
physics reduces to the totally quantified quantum physics. In
such a picture, everything becomes pure quantity which, at its
simplest, means a binary code. Where science provides the
intellectual parallel, technology manifests the practical aspect
of the drive towards complete quantification. The computer,
based on purely quantified data and instructions, is the machine
equivalent to a quantum physics, operating on discrete bits of
information.

   The history of technology can be viewed as a series of steps
towards replacing human functions by machine equivalents.
The earliest technologies, such as weaving and carving (I have
referred to these as the craft tools) were performed by the action
of the hand, powered by the human muscle and governed by the
human mind. Such simple technologies were extended by
prosthetic devices, such as the wheel and the plough; the human

muscle was supplemented by the use of animals. However, the ox-drawn plough is still a sacred technology linked to a ritualistic expression of the craftsman's relationship with nature and with God. There is little abstraction involved in extending the hand by the spade and further by the plough, but there is some. A ploughman working a field will have a different relationship to the land than will a gardener. The horse-drawn cart changes the sense of distance, of space, from that sensed by walking. So even the simplest forms of mechanization reduce phenomena to some degree, highlight the quantitative in contrast to the qualitative. The plough digs up *more* field than the spade and the spade more than the bare hands. It is more efficient. Nevertheless the religious constraints on the technology, the craft as a ritual, keep that move towards quantification within bounds.

Mechanization took a grip on society as muscle power gave way to wind and water. The water-mill and windmill could do even more work than animal-powered tools could possibly manage. The invention of the steam engine and the importing of gunpowder to the West then enabled man to have tools powered by fully controllable mechanized sources. No longer did the rain have to supply water or the winds have to blow, steam and explosives could provide power whenever it was convenient to man. The bonds had been loosened further and man gained more 'control', more power over nature. A shift had been made from having dominion over nature (that is being a responsible and loving landlord) to dominating nature. Such a shift can be expressed as a turn from the positive connotations of dominion, to its negative attributes. Such a shift gave man the sense of being independent of nature, it allowed a quantitative technology to be approached. Mechanization increased still further with the invention of the internal combustion engine and the development of electric power. New industries grew alongside the changing technology and the development of electric power. Jobs became routine, automatic even, as the web of a complex technological society was formed.

This independence from nature also meant more uniformity. People travelled further, places began to look alike as railways and roads spread their form of repetitive sameness across the countryside. This uniformity, this development of mass culture, mass education, mass movements, paralleled the development of statistical thought in science, which itself was bred from the new technology. The drive towards quantity, towards reduction to number, stemmed from man's abstraction from nature, his increasing mastery of the elements, a mastery that mechanization was producing. Nature itself became something to be used, and used increasingly to enhance the material wealth of the new society. Uniformity was only part of the price paid for the increase in wealth; the rapid decline of spiritual value that accompanied the rise of material benefits is a cost that modern economists never put into the equation. The fact that such a value is barely remarked upon as missing from our lives today is in itself a measure of how much we have paid for the apparent gains.

Peter Marsh has shown that all activities are combinations of power, action and control. The technologies described so far have been concerned with mechanizing the source of power and the action thereby produced, for example the rotation of the miller's grindstone. In all the craft technologies, the control device was the human, but the origins of modern science and technology began with the mechanical clock, the first device to be machine- or self-controlled. From the introduction of the clock until the real origins of computing technology in the nineteenth century, control of machines was kept as a human activity. During the nineteenth century, however, conveyor belt techniques arose that allowed semi-automation of biscuit making, meat packing and eventually the assembly line concept of production. In these cases some of the control, that had been a purely human prerogative, was handed over to machinery.

At the beginning of the nineteenth century a Frenchman named Joseph Marie Jacquard developed a weaving loom controlled by information coded on punched cards. This single development not only set the course of the computer revolution yet to come but was a significant step on the path towards the embodiment of a purely quantitative technology, one where man neither controlled nor powered his tools and in which was embodied an abstract notion of the world. The Jacquard loom remains the basis of modern automatic looms; it revolutionized the weaving industry, putting control firmly into the hands of the loom owners, rather than those of the weavers, and was an important part of the industrialization of the Western World. It is perhaps no more than a footnote to add that Jacquard fought on the side of the revolutionaries in the French Revolution, presumably adding to the tendency of the revolutionaries to want to redefine nature for the convenience of man and to set aside all traditions. The invention of the metric system of units by the French was a move towards an abstract quantification and away from a humanly based and qualitative system of sacred measures. Incidentally the Jacquard loom, born of a movement towards democracy, was one of the prime technologies that helped establish a capitalist-based industry.

The Jacquard loom was at least one of the factors that influenced Charles Babbage, who can rightly be called the father of modern computers. Babbage had the idea that a machine could be built that could calculate any required mathematical tables, and do so accurately. His paper, presented to the Royal Astronomical Society in 1822, was entitled 'Observations on the Application of Machinery to the Computation of Mathematical Tables' and Babbage accompanied the paper by the demonstration of a working model of the proposed device. For eleven years Babbage, funded mainly by government grants, struggled to realize his machine in a working prototype, but the accuracy required for fashioning the innumerable components could not be achieved with the tools and skills of the day. However, Babbage also lost interest in his Difference Engine because another idea had occurred to him that really gave birth to computers as we know them. Babbage expanded on his ideas of a machine that could produce any required mathematical tables to one that could perform any calculation you could think of. His Analytical Engine, the first concept of a universal computer, was never built, although parts of it were made, but its design was essentially that of a present-day computer, consisting of input, output and a processing mill as well as a memory store. What Babbage had conceptualized and attempted to make was nothing short of a machine in which abstract models of reality, expressed in terms of quantities, were manifest in hardware and software.

The story of Babbage and his two loves, the Analytical Engine and Ada, Countess of Lovelace, is nowadays well known.

The romance has a sad ending, for Ada died at the age of thirty-six as Babbage's fortunes were falling. She had both encouraged his work and immortalized it in her Notes, which she called 'Observations on Mr. Babbage's analytical engine'. Without those his work would never have been given the importance it was to have a hundred years later, for Babbage himself wrote down nothing about his machine. The parts he built are preserved in museums but, without Ada's notes, would mean little. Her death and his inability to build a computer a century ahead of its time led Babbage to die a disappointed and unfulfilled man in 1871. His esteem, however, indeed his recognized genius, led to a curious parody of Babbage's thought and work. He had not been merely an eccentric inventor but was a highly regarded mathematician, at one time Lucasian Professor of Mathematics at Cambridge University, and Fellow of the Royal Society. When he died his brain was removed and preserved in specimen jars. The surgeons of the day wanted to see what physical signs his brain might show of his genius. None were discovered but the brain is still to be seen in the museum of the Royal College of Surgeons in London. The man who first thought of a machine that acted like a disembodied brain had his own brain disembodied, and displayed, like his processing mill that never 'thought', in a museum.

Within fifty years of Babbage's death four men had been born who were to bring the notion of a universal computer to fruition. They were Vannevar Bush, Konrad Zuse, Howard Aiken and Alan Turing. Of course, in addition to these men were many others whose contributions both theoretical and practical to the development of computers were significant. Bush extended the mechanical techniques, begun by Jacquard and Babbage, to their limits. The MIT differential analyser, which he built in the early 1930s, although electrically driven, was essentially a mechanical, cogs and wheels, device. It was set up to calculate differential equations in order to solve ballistics problems for testing the capability of weapons. It was not fully a computer, neither matching Babbage's specification nor fitting the definition given here in Chapter 2, but, despite its decimal notation rather than binary quantification, it was a clear contender for being considered amongst the first computers.

Zuse built his machines to operate with a binary notation. His insight into simple switching devices representing binary digits, combined with his skills at pioneering new engineering techniques, makes him a key figure in the 1930s and '40s. Zuse was a young genius. He built his first computer, the Z1, on the sitting-room table in his parents' house in Germany. By 1941 he had built the Z3, the first fully operational electro-mechanical computer. The short-sightedness of Nazi funding policies meant that Zuse computers were never sufficiently developed during World War Two, although his own firm was later incorporated into the Siemens empire.

At the same time as Zuse was working in Germany, Howard Aiken at Harvard University in the USA had realized that a fully universal computer was a conceptually different thing from a large complex of calculating machines, such as were made and marketed to most large government and commercial offices. Seeking financial support from IBM, he built the machine that was later called the Harvard Mark 1. It was a huge machine, part electrical and part mechanical, and it was constructed for and operated by the US Navy, again in order to calculate ballistic trajectories for the development of weapons. The Mark 1 was certainly the first machine to be called an 'electronic brain' although its claim to be the first is not fully justified.

In Britain, working under top secrecy, Alan Turing, together with a team that included I. J. Good and Donald Michie, had built and were operating a fully electronic computer called Colossus. This machine, which was fully operational before the end of 1943, was sited at Bletchley Park and was dedicated to cracking the Enigma codes the Germans were using for their military intelligence. It is this latter fact, that Colossus was not a universal computer but designed as an electronic code-cracking machine, that prevents it from being regarded as the first real computer. The Mark 1 was a better fit to Babbage's ideal. However Colossus was effectively the first electronic computer and Turing, whose theoretical work in the 1930s led to its development, is probably more in line as Babbage's successor than the other three men. What Babbage had initiated in 1822 was brought to final fruition in 1946, when ENIAC was launched on the world. The first fully electronic, general-purpose computer had been built.

The men who built ENIAC were John Mauchly and J. Presper Eckert, both from the Moore School of Electrical Engineering at the University of Pennsylvania, and although they designed the machine for the US Army Ordnance Corps, again to calculate ballistic trajectories, the machine could be programmed to perform any computation. At least, it could be re-programmed with some difficulty, because the program was wired into the machine through switches, plug-boards and cables and to change it required considerable reorganization of those components. The mathematician John Von Neumann was introduced to ENIAC in its early stages of construction, indeed, he worked on the project himself, and realized that the limitations of the machine's programmability could be solved if program instructions could be treated like any other data, reduced to numbers and stored inside the machine. This concept, which added the final degree of flexibility to computer design, was incorporated into the design of the Moore School's second computer EDVAC, which was never completed as Eckert and Mauchly left to set up their own company. The idea was built into their machine, BINAC, which appeared in 1950, but by then Kilburn and Williams had incorporated stored programming into the Manchester Mark 1 and so had Maurice Wilkes at Cambridge with his EDSAC machine.

Von Neumann, whose interests and work led him to play a key role in the development of the hydrogen bomb, had realized that a computer was essential for advanced work in applied nuclear physics. ENIAC, although used for ten years by the US Army, did not satisfy Von Neumann's demands and he contributed to the mathematical basis for a giant computer which was built at Princeton. Interestingly enough, the Princeton machine was copied at Los Alamos for the bomb project and Von Neumann suggested that that machine should be named MANIAC.

From then on, more and more machines were constructed. The first machine used in commerce was LEO, made for the Lyons Teashop Company in London, and in the USA giant corporations, like IBM, Sperry Rand, and Bell Telephone, moved into the computer field. The machines somehow lost the personal touch that the early pioneers had given to their constructions although, as Tracy Kidder has shown in his book *The Soul of a New Machine*, in which he follows the development of a new Data General mini-computer, there is still excitement and a human story to be found in the development of a present-day computer.

The origins of microtechnology began, then, with Babbage, who originated the concept of a universal computing machine. Coming at a time in history when the quantification of the world was increasing dramatically, Babbage added to this tendency by conjuring up the notion of a machine that 'thinks', turning human thought and reasoning ability to numbers that could be operated on by a machine. Even then, there were limitations, as Ada wrote in her notes. The Analytical Engine might be able to do anything asked of it, that could be programmed into it, but it could not 'create', it could have 'no pretensions whatever to *originate* anything' as she said herself (her italics). When we reach Turing in the mid-twentieth century (his paper 'Computing Machinery and Intelligence' was published in 1950) such restrictions have disappeared. Turing not only suggested that machines could be built that would 'learn', but he discusses a 'child-machine', which, being analogous to a child, would have to be programmed to learn as a child does, both formally and by experience. His ambition was to see, he thought by the end of the twentieth century, machines that could 'compete with man in all purely intellectual fields'.

It is worth quoting Turing to illustrate his own particular style of thought.

Instead of trying to produce a programme to simulate the adult mind, why not rather try to produce one which simulates the child's? If this were then subjected to an appropriate course of education one would obtain the adult brain. Presumably the child-brain is something like a notebook as one buys it from the stationers. Rather little mechanism and lots of blank sheets. (Mechanism and writing are from our point of view almost synonymous.) Our hope is that there is so little mechanism in the child-brain that something like it can be easily programmed. The amount of work in the education we can assume, as a first approximation, to be much the same as for the human child.

He continues: 'We cannot expect to find a good child-machine at the first attempt. One must experiment with teaching one such machine and see how well it learns. One can then try another and see if it is better or worse. There is an obvious connection between this process and evolution'.

This passage illustrates the reductionist attitude towards man and human thought, in that nothing other than data, which could be quantified, and mechanisms for handling that data are seen in human life. To see a child's brain, and hence its mind, as akin to a notebook is permissible as a simple allegory of a particular kind, but then to replicate the child, and thence the adult, by using the notebook simile is pure reductionism. Further than that, Turing also demonstrates the attitude towards nature that epitomized the same mode of thought and which is concerned with mastery over nature. He is suggesting that by experimenting with various models of child-machine, one can simulate the natural processes of evolution in creating a form of species. Norman Moss called the builders of the hydrogen bomb the 'Men who play God' but the same mentality, at the same time in history, is shown explicitly here, although in apparent innocence. What is sought is the supremacy of man, not man the human being, but man the machine.

The reductionist attitude, the paring down of all existence to bare number, even further, paring down all number to merely one and zero, something and nothing, may seem extreme and yet it is encapsulated in the very tools that are rapidly surrounding us, in the hardware and software of computing technology. Quantification without bounds becomes extreme because it leaves out so much.

If the parents of computer technology are to be found in the philosophy of reductionism, the midwife was certainly the military, and capital-based industry was the nurse. The Harvard Mark 1, Colossus and ENIAC were built for purposes of warfare, and the mentality of military strategists, who regard people as dead or live pieces of meat, to be counted in terms of megadeaths, tallies nicely with the mentality of the men of 'genius' who built the machines to help kill people more efficiently. Weapons are designed to kill people, that is their task, and no excuse is provided by the afterthought that it was not expected that the weapons would be used. Victorians expressed their attitude to heredity by saying that someone who went astray had 'bad blood'. The computer was born with 'bad blood' and, as its developments are still inextricably bound up with the military, the argument cannot be accepted that it has transcended its origins. The symbolism of events is powerful and significant and the origins of computers cannot be passed off as being technically interesting and morally neutral. The symbolism expressed in MANIAC, just as in the acronym for the NATO policy of Mutually Assured Destruction—MAD—is far more than a joke, it is a true expression of the reality of the thing.

Allied to the military complex are the huge capitalistic industries, whose multi-national scale of enterprise outstrips most national governments. The new empires are commercial and the computer is central to their operation and as their product. The irony of the modern movements away from the personal tyranny of the feudal barons towards democracy, freedom and equality is that the capitalism that replaced feudalism concentrates power into far fewer hands than did its despotic predecessor. Today, much of the world is effectively influenced by the few faceless barons of industry, voted for only by the shareholders, and whose interests are their own first and the public's only in so far as the public interest serves that of their corporation. In communist countries the capital-based, technological industries serve the interest of the state, rather than the corporation, but the effect is the same. Despite their different surface politics, the direction of all the developed nations is firmly founded on their technological base, and the direction is towards a greater materialism and secularization. In the USSR and in the USA religion thrives for a minority who are tolerated in different ways by the technocracy. The web of power the interconnected corporations have built up has been achieved through the electric and electronic technologies. As McLuhan said, electric media extend the nervous system, and the network of electric media around the globe has used that aspect of the extension of man to create the dependency of the people on big business. Attempts to break that web, to find alternative technologies, to go organic, are crushed by the power of the corporations.

There seems to be an implicit conspiracy between governments and the military/industrial complex to tighten their grip on the world by the rapid development of any and every technology available. The two most powerful technologies for doing that, both of which emerged from the 1930s, are television and computers. Both redefine the world in unreal terms; one by presenting selected images of things and claiming they are 'real', extracting from the rich reality of experience only those ingredients that make for compelling viewing; the other redefines the world by reducing it to numbers. The motivation is to gain complete control of the world. The notion of a colony in space is a current goal that indicates that aim of a totally controlled environment. The intellectual backing for such an enterprise is the science that accompanies the technology, that acts as the tool to achieve the end. The philosophy is reductionism and eventually nihilism, for reductionism finally reduces everything to nothing. It is a total secularization of the world, squeezing God out of every corner until nothing is left but what man has selected or placed there.

The bleakness and extremity of this view of the origin and direction of microtechnology is often countered by the idea that the new technology, being flexible, allowing individual differences, being soft rather than hard, can take us in quite a new direction. So Margaret Boden, for instance, in her scholarly work *Artificial Intelligence and Natural Man* concludes by saying: 'the prime metaphysical significance of artificial intelligence is that it can *counteract* the subtly dehumanizing influence of natural science, of which so many cultural critics have complained.' What is not sufficiently appreciated, as far as I can see, is that the new flexible, soft technologies are not a new departure, but a subtle extension of the same thing. The approach may no longer be mechanistic, but it is still reductionist and still springs from the mentality that began by leading down the mechanistic path. The recognition that the new technology is the old one extended and disguised in new clothing enables us to choose neither of the two options offered by Christopher Evans or Margaret Boden. Evans, recalling the film *Things to Come*, sets up the alternatives between taking the path of knowledge that science opens up, wherever that leads (note the objective path of science) or else 'live with the insects in the dust'. Margaret Boden's alternatives are similar, if less picturesque. She writes: 'We must either deny our humanity, with socially destructive results, or else forfeit a scientific understanding of the world in general and people in particular'. Phrased like that there seems to be no option but to pursue modern science and technology wherever it (or the military/industrial complex) leads. These stark alternatives are, however, propaganda for the technological imperative and nothing more. There are other alternatives in which our humanity is not denied nor are we forced to follow a technological path born of warfare and whose end is to evolve machines to replace people.

The flexible, soft technology, as we shall see in Chapter 9, can tighten its grip on society far more comprehensively than did the rigid, mechanical sort. The subtlety of approach deceives, just like the spider's web. The origins of computing technology spring from that attitude to the world that struggles to reduce everything to number; it has been shown in earlier chapters how that is practised in computers. The link between computing technology and technology and science in general has been drawn in. The base of the technology lies in Western materialistic society and the futures that have been conjectured extend that society further into pure materialism. The effect the technology is having now on society and on the individual we look at next, but the effects we shall examine derive from the origins of the technology. The technological mirror of our age reflects the image of MANIAC.

8 COMPUTERS AND WORK

The world is being redefined in terms of information. There is an information explosion, which is brought about partly by the acceleration of processes that can be traced back to the changes that gave rise to the industrial revolution (though some claim the origins lie in the early history of the planet) and partly by the technology that processes information and thereby turns things into yet more information. To expand this latter point first, we have already seen how a universal information-processing machine, especially when reduced in size and cost, can transform any other machine or operation into one that is powerful and flexible and concerned fundamentally with information. The chip-controlled machine-tool processes the information of an idea into its realization. The product is not important, it is the information and its flow and amplification that counts. In this way, all manufacturing and service operations can be turned primarily into information systems. The accelerating impetus of the technology results, therefore, in an explosion of information.

The historical build-up of information can be assessed visually in academic libraries, where the shelf space required for the steadily accumulating journals increases every year. A journal from the 1930s may occupy two or three inches for one year's volume, while by the 1970s the same journal may spread over fifteen or twenty inches for an annual series of editions. However, information is more than just the accumulation of books and journals on library shelves, it is found in diverse forms; computer output, newspapers, broadcasting, tele-communications, postal services, teaching, government, in-dustrial and commercial operations, accounting, stock listing, transport . . . the list is endless. In all areas where information is the central 'product', it is growing in volume continually.

The industrial revolution was brought about not only by the new technology of the day, but also by the development of trade and commerce, the rise of the importance of information. What happened in that revolution was that machines were sub- stituted for muscle power and some human skills and gave rise to a new economy, an information-based one. The concentra- tion of power into the hands of industrialists came about through the separation of information, which was the province of management, from the skills of the work-force and their ability to control machines. As Juan Rada wrote in *The Impact of micro-electronics*, 'This development was in conformity with a more profound tendency of capital to become as independent as possible of the human factors that condition its reproduction' (p. 8). An economy geared to increased growth can achieve its aims more readily if information is the main resource, for it is an inexhaustible resource and one that can continue to increase in value the more it is circulated. Hence, an argument can be pieced together explaining the information explosion as the rapid acceleration of the tendency of modern economies to grow. The new technology aids this end by replacing human skills almost entirely, liberating the forces that generate wealth from the restrictions of human fallibility, frailty and unreliabil- ity. Without doubt this latest stage in technological develop- ment is a major turning point, so much so that other commen- tators link it to the processes of biological evolution.

The emergence of man has been linked to the property of mammalian brains that can store more information than can their genes. So man emerges, in this evolutionary picture, as an information-processing animal (about which I shall comment in a later chapter). The invention of writing then enabled man to store more information in libraries than could be stored in his brain; microtechnology, finally, allows 'intelligence' to be stored and amplified in an artificial form, independent of and external to man himself. Hence brains exceeded genes, libraries exceeded brains, and computers exceeded libraries, in this scenario. Stated like that it seems a naïve and rather sparse sequence, but it has two points of interest. First, the time-scale of the stages in the sequence dramatizes the explosion aspect of information growth, with advances taking millions of years, thousands of years and finally tens of years to take place. Also, the sequence shows a move towards abstraction in the notebook of those who propose such ideas. However, this link between computing technology and evolutionary progress is one that will reappear when we discuss artificial intelligence in Chapter 10. Daniel Bell, in a not dissimilar approach, has outlined four stages towards an information society, namely speech, writing, printing and telecommunications. Again each stage is a further abstraction from the previous one.

What is not in doubt is that the new means for data storage and retrieval, and for information processing is transforming commercial, governmental and industrial practices and thereby transforming society. Projections of leisured societies, of paperless offices, of cashless banks are all scenarios for what is so frequently discussed as the 'new' society that is expected to emerge as developed countries move into a post-industrial phase of development. What that means, of course, is that whereby industrialization meant that products were the main concern, in the 'new' society information will be the key resource, the essential resource. The growth not only of computers but also of communications networks has meant that the information industries encompass the globe and their impact needs careful assessment, because more and more industries are being turned into information concerns. This is a new revolution, on a scale unprecedented, and it is only just beginning to be felt. Data transmission has increased twelve-fold in the past ten years in Europe. More than half the gross national product of the United States comes from the inform-ation industry. The trends are illustrated in these unrefined facts; information is the essential resource of the newly emerging society.

The impact of these changes is felt most abruptly in the effects new technology has on employment and the nature of work, but the repercussions will be felt throughout society as a whole. In the following chapter I shall discuss the more general social effects that arise from the control and flow of information and society's dependence on it; here we continue by looking at the impact of computers on work, brought about by the transformation of all machines into information processors.

Discussion and predictions about the effects of microtechno-logy on employment are always and necessarily prefaced with a caution that what is to follow is speculative and uncertain. For authors to give such a warning is correct, for only the first signs of future trends are available for analysis and the factors that affect employment are numerous and complex. The fact that unemployment in the developed countries is high and still rising (at the time of writing) is due to more than new technology. For a decade there has been a recession and society has been adjusting to new trade patterns, the effects of price control of oil and other resources, and changing balances in world monetary systems. To separate out the individual factors that lead to variations in employment statistics is just not possible and only trends can be discerned and suspicions voiced. I join others in warning, therefore, that predictions given here, and the establishment of apparent patterns, are based on my own speculations about what will happen in the future. What I have tried to do is base opinion on present facts and to tie my own speculations on as sound a theoretical base as I can. That theoretical base is the notion, already described, that technology springs from a particular attitude to the world that is linked closely to the developed countries' form of economy, namely capitalism; both competitive, market-place capitalism epitomized by Japan and the USA, and state capitalism as practised in the Iron Curtain countries. Such economies are based on a technology that separates information from skill, and which always seeks either a well controlled work-force or its replacement by more reliable machines; thus the new technology enables technocratic control to be exercised even more strongly and offers another means for the replacement of the 'human factor' in the wealth generation process. The technology is not neutral, hence its effects can be predicted (maybe not very reliably) on the basis of what it represents. That is the line I pursue here.

In manufacturing industries, the introduction of the microchip, robots and automation affects the products and processes in several ways. Products are improved or transformed and new products are created. Examples are the chip-monitored car, which improves its performance and safety, the digital watch that has transformed the watchmaking industry and the calculator and electronics games which have opened up quite new markets. Hazardous work can be performed and dangerous working environments can be operated in by robots, relieving the human worker from conditions that threaten health and life. The monotonous and repetitive tasks, so frequently described as mindless, can be taken over by machines, so that jobs can be cleaner, safer, more interesting. Computer control can improve management efficiency, reduce energy losses, monitor and prevent unacceptable pollution levels and in several ways contribute to higher productivity. However, all these things come at the expense of at least some jobs.

Automation always implies a reduction in the labour force. New technology is not installed for purely technical reasons, but almost entirely for economic ones. The machine can produce more, and more reliably, than the men it replaces. It is when the cost of the machine begins to equal the cost of the labour it will replace that it becomes very attractive to industry. The increased productivity of the capital intensive, new technology factory makes it more competitive than the older, mechanized firms, hence stimulating more automation and more job losses. That is the tendency. In addition, the smaller firms are less able to afford the capital expense, lack a true competitive edge and hence go bankrupt, leading to further job losses. Their share of the market then falls to the automated high-technology businesses, which do not need to take on more labour to increase their productivity still further; so the jobs are lost for good, at least from that sector of industry. Unfortunately, this tendency applies to more and more sectors of the overall industrial scene. The classic example of the process is the watch industry.

Traditionally, the making of mechanical clocks and watches was almost a cottage industry, with hundreds of small firms and craftsmen making various components, assembling units, finishing, decorating and so on. The industry was craft-based and labour intensive. Marketing was largely through the jeweller's shop, and watches and clocks were normally regarded as quality products. The introduction of electronic timepieces in Japan and the United States dramatically affected the Swiss and German clock and watch industry. Reluctance to adopt new technology, new marketing methods and new methods of production meant that between 1970 and 1977 the Swiss industry lost nearly half of its share of the world market and reduced its labour force by 40 per cent. The number of jobs lost by the Federal Republic of Germany's clock industry, over the same time-span, was 14,000—44 per cent of its total number of workers. That trend has continued into the 1980s as the proportion of electronic digital watches has increased to around 60 per cent of the world market. The decline of watchmaking continues, though not so dramatically as in the early seventies. In addition, the new technology watches and clocks are mass marketed through chain stores, mail order and the new technology shops rather than through the older-style jewellers' shops, so the impact has been felt not only by the manufacturers, but also by the retailers.

If the traditional watch industry provides an example of the failure to adapt to new technologies, with resultant loss of jobs and a smaller slice of the market, the car industry illustrates the way that fully automated manufacturing processes also lead to fewer jobs. The Fiat Robogate factory, which makes cars untouched by human hand, is designed to weld one car body every minute. A central computer controls the handling of components, their transport to assembly and welding robots, the quality control checks and more. The system can handle two different car models at once and a switch of program enables an even wider range of models to be constructed on the same process line.

Industrial robots are now used for car manufacture in Sweden, Germany, France, and Britain as well as in Japan and the USA. Indeed, in Japan around 30,000 robots are employed in motor car manufacture alone. Estimates put the cost effectiveness of these machines at half the price of human labour and some estimates forecast that by 1990 between 5 and 10 per cent of the labour force in manufacturing industry as a whole will have been replaced by robot labour. The effect of automation in the automobile industry is to increase the competitiveness of an already very competitive trade. Car costs have to be held to a minimum in order to maintain a market presence. The British car industry has declined over the past decade partly because of fierce competition from other European and Japanese car makers, whose investment in automation has made some impact on the price of their product. So effective has been the Japanese industry, that even in the United States the local industry has felt the pinch.

What is referred to as 'flexible manufacturing' extends the

same principle to small units in industry, enabling the manufacture of a wide range of products in small batches through computer-controlled production lines. The result is to remove workers from production, replacing them with robots, leaving a small number, possibly even only one person, to control the overall operation. Such schemes are costly in terms of capital investment but, in the UK, government grants help significantly towards setting up flexible manufacturing plants. Programmable general-purpose robots are also being developed which will contribute to the automation of smaller-scale industry. Robots are now being built by robots so their price is falling, increasing their impact on the current industrial revolution. Already programmable robots are used for product assembly, for example, putting together the seventeen parts of engine alternators in less than three minutes, completely outstripping human performance. Productivity is evaluated in terms of the ratio of output to costs, and can be increased either by increasing output or by decreasing costs. Automation can certainly increase output and will also decrease costs once the capital expenditure is written off. As labour costs increase and robot prices fall automation rapidly becomes more attractive to the large-scale manufacturer but it also comes within the financial sights of the smaller industrial concern.

Levels of employment, like productivity, are a balance between two factors; jobs lost versus new jobs created. So far we have looked at areas of job loss, which have been the traditional industries and the increasingly automated manufacturing plants. Microtechnology has created new industries, however, and rapidly increased the scale and importance of all the electronics-based firms. The computer industry has grown dramatically since the 1950s and so has the consumer electronics sector (TVs, radios, calculators, TV games, electronic kitchen products, etc.). Office technology, switching from mechanical to electronic, is another growth area as is point-of-sale equipment (computer-based cash registers, etc.) and telecommunications systems. From the mid-1960s to mid-1970s the electronics market grew by over 200 per cent, and in every industrialized country outstripped increases in gross national product. The range of electronic products also jumped dramatically: Olivetti's catalogue listed 95 products in 1965 and over

600 in 1978, so growth in this area has been consistent and still continues.

Whilst traditional industries, like steelmaking and shipbuilding, have declined in recent years, the new industries have grown, based on the new technology. The argument is commonly presented that new industries, creating more wealth, inevitably create more jobs as well. It has been so in the past, but the past is not always a reliable indicator of the present. Job creation in the nineteenth century came about with new labour-intensive industries, like the railways; but it frequently involved importing the labour and ultimately meant transferring people from one occupation, say agriculture, to another. Comparing one industry with another does not necessarily give a good overall picture and the comparison of past with present also needs to take into account the nature of the technology. So the question to ask is whether the new growth industries follow the past trends of promoting jobs?

The electronics industry is, as might be expected, the most technically advanced and most automated of all industries, so its growth has been in terms of output rather than in terms of jobs created. There has even been job loss whilst growth in output has been spectacular. In 1977, for example, the West German computer industry increased its production by 27.8 per cent whilst reducing its personnel by 4 per cent. During the 1970s, major electronics equipment makers reduced the number of their employees by as much as 40 per cent with most of the reduction affecting the less skilled workers. Job creation has been largely in the technical and development side of the industrial process, software development accounting for the major increase in job opportunity. However more jobs are being lost than gained.

The new jobs created in industry and commerce, promoted by the new technology, are largely for computer programmers. Because this is an area of expanding job opportunity, educational policies are being promoted to persuade children and young people to train in computer programming. Schools are encouraged through subsidies and promotional literature to purchase small computers and parents focus their concern on ensuring that children get the opportunity to learn about computers. This may seem very encouraging, except that the main effort in computer programming research is now being directed towards developing programs that write programs and for programs to have the ability to program themselves. In computing circles it is recognized that the age of high demand for the computer programmer will be very short and those jobs will equally rapidly disappear.

Many new firms have been created in the past decade, based on developing new electronic products, micro-computers and their peripherals, with subsequent job creation opportunities. However, such enterprise has only succeeded in a small number of cases. Once the market for a successful new product has been created the large companies take over; with greater development and marketing resources they can dominate the small firms and put them out of business. There are success stories, of course, but for each one there are many more failures. The employment opportunities opened up by new companies being formed has little if any effect on overall employment statistics.

In past times of technical change the loss of jobs from industrial mechanization has resulted in an increase in the service industries and a redistribution of employment. The increasing complexity of industrial societies has always meant more opportunity for clerical and administrative work and, as personal disposable income has increased, so there has been an expansion of the personal service sector. The new technology, being electronic rather than mechanical, capital rather than labour intensive and primarily concerned with information processing, has affected the service industries as well.

The office revolution is perhaps the most dramatic example of the way microtechnology is having an impact on service industries, but the repercussions from automating many administrative, communications and personal service operations amount to a greater social impact than in the manufacturing sector. As an example, consider the implications of electronic mail and telecommunications for facsimile transmission (transferring documents electronically from a 'reader' to a printer elsewhere), automatic meter reading, tele-conferencing (round-table discussions with participants in different locations) and view-data services. All these operations, based on micro-electronics, are coming into use in Britain and the USA and are expected to be in full use before 1990, including home printing of electronically transmitted newspapers.

Electronic mail dispenses with the traditional postman, or at least reduces the hand-delivered postal service considerably, for there will still be some need for the physical transfer of documents, parcels and so on. Automatic mail sorting has already cut down the number of postal workers and the introduction of the electronic transfer of information will reduce the service still more. However, the impact will spread somewhat further. Allied to the postal service are printing, stationery production, stamp making (design, printing, distribution) and several other businesses. The small-scale printer of letter headings, the notepaper and envelope producers, the retail aspects of postal materials, will all suffer reduction in business and hence will either go bankrupt or will have to shed personnel in order to remain viable. Automatic meter reading dispenses with the meter reader and also reduces the human labour in sorting and administering the paperwork associated with the processing of electric and gas service meters. Facsimile transmission extends the impact of electronic mail, whilst tele-conferencing also affects transport services.

The newspaper industry has been beset with difficulties for many years, partly due to changing economics and also due to the introduction of new technology. As mentioned before, it is now possible for a journalist to type his story on a keyboard, edit the text and automatically have the product photo-typeset ready for printing without the necessity for other staff. Several traditional jobs have simply disappeared. If news material is then electronically transmitted and reproduced within the home, then even the final printing of newspapers would be removed and the industry transformed beyond recognition. It is no surprise that the unions connected with the newspaper industry have been resisting such changes or accommodating them only with tough conditions attached, for the impact of the new technology on jobs has been felt keenly.

As with manufacturing industries, the growth of microtechnology-based service industries such as banking is not accompanied by a corresponding increase in new jobs, for these industries, by their nature, are highly automated. Their spread, accompanied by increased centralization, is already leading to a net loss of jobs, difficulties for small firms to remain competitive, and frequently a loss of service to the customer.

The introduction of electronic funds transfer and automatic banking will mean an inevitable loss of jobs in banking and accountancy as the computer will handle transactions currently being handled manually. The millions of cheques now passing between banks daily will disappear, again affecting printing, stationery and transport services, and the clerks now employed will no longer be required. The same story also applies to many of the routine clerical, accounting and other office work that is presently done manually. Insurance firms, government agencies and other centres of public and commercial administration are all transferring labour to machines.

The office revolution is centred on word processing and electronic filing, both of which activities appreciably increase the efficiency of secretarial work. With the earlier word-processing facilities, in the mid-1970s, it was generally found that use of a word processor increased secretarial productivity by between 100 and 150 per cent. Many firms and institutions found they could dispense with a large typing pool because of the additional power given to typists through the word processor. Typing is made faster because corrections are simple and quick to make, texts can be edited and do not need retyping in full and standard letter forms can be stored and modified for each specific use. The printer can be operating while the secretary is typing something else into the machine and it can still be printing when the operator is having a lunch break. With these more recent facilities built into the machine, productivity is increased threefold, which either means the work load of the office can be increased considerably, with no need for extra staff, or else staff can be cut back in number. Either way actual or potential jobs are lost.

Most secretarial work is performed by women so they are the first to suffer the effects of converting the office to the new technology. In West Germany, where there are around five million typist and secretarial jobs at present, it is reckoned that between 25 and 40 per cent of those jobs could be lost to office automation; that would affect nearly two million people. The *Wall Street Journal* reported in November 1982 that even in the professional and managerial jobs a disproportionate number of women are laid off when office automation encroaches into business. Women will also feel the effects of automation in other service industries as well as in manufacturing, particularly as it is more usual for part-time staff to be women and it will be those jobs that are shed first. Many employers prefer to give jobs to men, especially in the more technical professions, where educational background tends to favour a male majority. Women, in general, are less organized as a labour force, fewer belonging to trade unions than men, and frequently they are working to supplement family income rather than as the bread winner. Unemployment due to new technology will therefore have an impact on male/female roles in society, probably reinforcing traditional patterns. However, women are probably in a better position than most men to revitalize craft work, where creativity and individually-made pieces will always retain value, and to staff the likely increase in human services, where the capacity to relate to people will be required in the 'caring' professions.

Since 1980 the cost of electronic office equipment has fallen sufficiently to make a word processor a cheaper alternative than a secretary and the cost of such a machine is now around three to four times the cost of an electric typewriter. If an operator working with a word processor can now do the work of three typists for the price of less than two, then the motivation to automate, without great capital expense, is strong. When the word processor is part of a network that includes electronic storage of information, then the system becomes even more powerful, and attractive for executives or managers to use themselves, giving them direct access to the information they need without the use of filing clerks or secretarial help. Space is saved (no more filing cabinets), costs are reduced (less use and wastage of paper), and efficiency increased. The future office could well consist of executives with terminals and a few secretarial assistants. Such a vision is disturbing, not only because of the reduced employment, but also because the remaining positions are skilled and of high status. How does a young person then work his or her way up to the managerial position? Junior posts would be largely redundant, so not only women will be affected by the micro revolution but also young people.

Given the employment-replacing effect of microprocessor-based technology, the question remains: what will be the actual effect on employment levels? Developed countries at present have been facing rising unemployment, which in several places is as high as 10 to 15 per cent on a national scale. Some reports have forecast projections of 25 per cent unemployment by the mid- to late 1990s which, for Britain, would represent seven to eight million people. The social cost of such a situation, with its attendant problems of frustration, boredom and resentment, (the unemployed suffer higher rates of physical and mental ill health, higher suicide and crime rates than do those in work) might not be acceptable either to governments or to the populace. Educational programmes to counteract the effects of increased 'leisure' may not be regarded as acceptable substitutes for work. Education to alter public attitudes to work then raises questions of social control that will be deferred to the next chapter. However, it is worth commenting that the so-called Protestant work ethic, which many regard as the attitude that needs to be altered, is the attitude that built up the system of industry and commerce whose goal was competitive productivity and economic growth. It was the attitude that gave rise to the technology that makes it redundant. I do not see how a society, based on such an attitude, could also exist as a 'leisured' society. The technology itself is 'work'-oriented.

One possible way out of the employment problem would be to reduce the size of the population, either dramatically by war, or else by a vigorous programme of birth control. Both methods raise any number of moral and ethical issues and neither offers any real solution to the problem of what people ought to do with their lives. Such an answer certainly reduces human worth by treating people either as objects that can be simply eliminated or as animals that need a controlled breeding programme. The solution is a technical 'fix' that assumes that the continuation of present technological developments is more important than the value of being human; that the products of work are more worthwhile than the process of doing the work. Certainly population size is one factor that determines the number of unemployed, but so too is the form of the economy and the social perception of the value of work.

The extent of unemployment due to new technology will

depend both on loss of jobs and the creation of new ones. One area where the balance tilts towards increased unemployment is in the loss of potential jobs created by micro-electronics. If we assume further economic growth, even at slow rates, then greater output is also assumed. In the past more output was generally a sign of more job opportunity but that is no longer the case. Already it is plain that new jobs are not being generated and even job replacement, due to retirement, resignation and promotion within organizations, is not occurring because of the increased productivity the technology provides. A decade ago the large commercial companies, banks and insurance firms, as well as governmental agencies recruited large numbers of school leavers into trainee and junior posts. That is no longer the case. In the UK banks cut back their staff by over 50,000 in the 1970s and in Germany reductions of 6 to 10 per cent were made in staffing levels. Potential jobs are lost and new jobs created in insufficient number to compensate because the new growth areas are high-technology industries. The unpredictability of the picture means, however, that people will have to wait to see the outcome.

Juan Rada, in his report for the International Labour Office in Geneva, puts forward four different propositions which could act as counter-measures to the tendency towards greater unemployment induced by micro-electronics. They can be summarized thus:

1. Reduction in working hours
2. Creating new products
3. Incentives to small industry
4. Increased public services.

The first of these counter-measures could be implemented by reducing the working week, getting rid of overtime, introducing longer holidays and encouraging earlier retirement. All of these measures, which would need to be encouraged by a suitable education programme, could only work provided the shorter hours did not mean less income for the worker. It will not be easy to reduce the working week and pay people proportionally less, because, although that may seem fair to the employer, people work because they need the money. Not only that, the economy as a whole needs them to have money, for without it, how can they buy the goods being produced? So reducing unemployment by shortening working hours comes at the expense of increasing labour costs, which is no incentive to employers.

The vision many commentators have is of a work-sharing community, whereby people share jobs with each other, can opt for retirement at any stage in their life, opt back into work, return to education whenever it seems appropriate to do so, and so on. Another vision is of a 'leisured society', where no one needs to work, except for a minority, who work on relatively short shifts. In such a society everyone is paid a salary by the state which is evaluated according to the profitability of the whole community. The automated factories, it is argued, will be so productive that they can produce the wealth necessary for everyone to enjoy a high standard of living. Such a scheme would require enormous changes in public attitude and in the structure of society. The thing that worries me most about such a proposition, however, is that economically it would not work.

Money is symbolic of human labour, even when it has been reduced to moving electrons in some computer circuit. If money is generated by machine labour and then distributed to the non-working population to buy the goods the machines make, then the net result is that the machines will be working for nothing, the goods will be effectively given away. As only a proportion of the money people spend will be on goods, that means the goods will not only be free, they will be given away with money attached, they will have a negative price. How then will the factories produce a profit that can be shared amongst the population? The notion is quite absurd. Money cannot be 'created' out of nothing, which is the assumption the 'leisure society' is based on. Furthermore, the 'leisure society' would be based on large industries, which, because of the new social order, would have to give their profits away to a non-productive population. Where would their motivation to create wealth come from? Why should they hand their money to governments to share out? Why not just get rid of the surplus population? The social consequences of such a vision could become a nightmare.

Reducing working hours, without loss of income to the

worker, seems a remote possibility in the attempt to prevent technological unemployment. Creating new products to create new jobs is an alternative which we have already encountered. New products are invariably high-technology products or produced on highly automated systems, which do not employ many people. Only an increase in the labour-intensive 'cottage industry' style of working would reduce unemployment appreciably, and I suspect there will be an increase in craft work and self employment amongst local communities. Independence from the large corporations may be the only guarantee that people will find to prevent themselves from being replaced by a machine. A 'black' economy is already growing and could end up as a genuine alternative to the high-technology, centralized, industrial concerns.

Rada states that incentives to small businesses 'are based on the long-standing recognition of their economic importance and employment potential'. He goes on to point out that, not only do they not invest in small businesses, but large-scale industry and services are concentrating and centralizing, thus squeezing out the smaller concern. Even in Japan, where subcontracting to small firms was traditional practice, concentration of industry is happening partly because of automation. The small firm cannot compete in the same market as the giant corporation, where high investment and low labour costs give the giant concern the competitive edge. Again small firms need to turn to an alternative product and their own more personalized economy.

The final counter-measure against unemployment is the creation of more public service jobs, and yet it is in the government sector that office automation will have a major impact on job loss. There are certainly strong cases to be made for increasing the numbers of nurses, doctors, teachers, social workers, counsellors and other personal service workers, but such jobs are 'unproductive' in an economic system that puts value on material rather than human needs. Such services need to be paid for, which means imposing higher taxes on the wealth-generating new technology industries. Such a scheme, not unlike the paradoxical 'leisure society' scenario, does not seem feasible in a world of economic competition. There is no doubt we need more not less in the way of caring services, but to expect such jobs to be created is to expect the unlikely; all of which paints a rather gloomy prospect of a future with inevitable high unemployment and more social division, despite educational attempts to make it bearable or acceptable. Rada, in *Impact of Micro-electronics*, summarizes the position thus:

It would seem that a transition is taking place from a society with unemployment to one that no longer needs its full potential labour force to produce the necessary goods and services under current conditions of work. It is doubtful whether measures such as early retirement, shorter working hours, and the creation and development of small businesses and new products and services will have much effect on job creation. Nevertheless, the need to meet the educational, cultural and social needs inherent in such a transition, plus cultural resistance, could lead to job creation in some fields. A transition of this nature will not be free from turmoil while the population tries to adjust to new life styles. (p. 105)

The response of the trade unions to this threat of increased unemployment has been widely discussed and cases of industrial action against the introduction of new technology, for example in the newspaper industry, have occurred. The outcome of such action has usually been a renegotiation of working terms and conditions in exchange for, at least partial, acceptance of the technology. The alternative is often the closure of the business and consequently even more unemployment. New technology is a powerful anti-union tool and that may account for the generally muted response of unions towards it. New technology certainly represents to trade unionists what M. Laver has called the four Rs, redundancy, redeployment, retraining and reduced skills, yet new technology is rarely discussed as a central issue in industrial relations. When it is, the term Luddite is all too commonly to be found, as discussions concerning the ill effects of new technology are generally regarded as anti-progressive and therefore not just old-fashioned but somehow destructive. It is frequently argued that society has always adjusted to past technological change and it will do so this time, but such arguments are not based on any detailed analysis of the effects of technology, nor on careful definitions of the factors that make for social progress and human well-being. Rather it is assumed that change is always for the better just because it is different, which is an odd and entirely modern viewpoint. Certainly the effect of new technologies on labour has been understood for centuries, and there are many recorded cases of machines being broken up by employees or by local government officers in medieval times; even the Roman Emperor Vespasian opposed water power for fear that it would create unemployment. The assumption that the Luddites were wrong is part of modern prejudice.

If the tendency of new technology in the developed countries is to create more unemployment, then its effect on the poorer, developing countries will be to widen the divide between 'them and us', between north and south. The reason for this lies in the freedom from labour needs that automation represents. One of the prime assets of developing countries is a very cheap labour force but, once a firm has decided to automate, its requirement for cheap labour disappears and with it the motivation for 'aiding' developing countries by investing in their assets, by building factories overseas. The automated plant might just as well remain in the parent country, where highly skilled technical assistance is more readily available.

The result is that the poor countries lose their foreign exchange, their financial aid through investments and the attendant military aid. They also lose people who were teaching them skills, and their few highly trained people are more likely to drift to the West.

It is an automatic reaction to think this a bad thing, because it is part of current thinking to assume that economic growth and technological progress are prime objectives in life, but underdeveloped countries may be better off without the form of 'aid' that industrialized nations like to give them. The new technologies are not neutral and if they are withdrawn, on economic grounds, then that may be for the better on cultural grounds. Certainly it can be argued that developing nations can well do without technologies that produce social divisions, technical élites, and unemployed populations that have been concentrated unnaturally into shanty towns: Despite the propaganda that information technology will unite the world in its electronic web, the fact remains that the new technology will widen the gap between rich and poor, both within countries and between countries. This is not just because of the effects automation has on labour but is also due to the way micro-electronics changes the nature of work.

Modern work is increasingly work with machines, rather than with people. A typical 1930s power station would have had a moderate work-force of engineers, boilermen, controllers, labourers, and administrators. There would have been the usual working relationships between people engaged in the same business, and a reasonable amount of human interaction. A typical power station of the 1980s will be almost empty. The whole operation will be supervised by two or three people in a high-technology control room, with administration taken care of centrally. The technician's job will be to make sure the machinery is organizing itself correctly, and to take control only when an emergency occurs. The job is technical and the environment artificial, with little human contact. It is typical of the way new technology changes work.

The new office consists of people relating more to their keyboard and television monitor than to other people. Electronic networks will heighten the feeling of being cut off that working with machines engenders. The sameness of a computer terminal, its blandness, reduces the sharpness of many human faculties; it produces a dependency, almost an addiction, and it reduces critical ability, just as television does. The new working environment may be safer, less dirty, less noisy but it is also less human, more monotonous, increasingly isolated and very artificial. What effects these new conditions will have on physical and mental health has yet to be discovered. Certainly there is some concern about the effect of the continual use of terminals on eyesight, and there are known dangers in artificial environments for people susceptible to epilepsy. The physical and mental effects of television viewing, which also relate to computer operators, (which term increasingly includes almost everyone) have been outlined by Gerry Mander. Much of his evidence is based on the work of John Ott in the USA, on the harmful effects of the imbalance of radiations emanating from electric technology, which is only just being treated seriously by the medical profession. In Canada, however, legislation now restricts the hours of working at a computer terminal screen to five hours a day and to zero for pregnant women.

Isolation from real human contact is not conducive to mental health in general; people need people. Social isolation does lead to mental ill-health and the new technology certainly reduces work-forces to a minimum and intervenes between direct human interaction. Such loss of relationship will surely increase distress, not only due to environments at work, but also at home as homes become computerized and more services, entertainment and information can be obtained without stepping outside the door. The 'new' home, centred on the computer terminal with its window on the world, can lead to much greater social isolation. When the whole world is your neighbour and you can communicate remotely with anyone, anywhere, you are replacing a genuine community, real human contact, with some fantasy world of images. In such a setting you cannot function as a whole person. The electronic home removes people from people, breaks down communities and families still further and leads to an increased fear of the outside world. This tendency can already be seen in the United States, where townships, highly computerized, are being developed like siege cities. The hostile world outside is kept at bay and therefore becomes or seems more hostile. People confined to home, working via their terminal, shopping over the computer link, receiving information and entertainment through the TV screen, will become less able to cope with direct human situations. Their humanity will have been lessened by the machine. What moral and spiritual effects such a redefined way of life would have can only be imagined.

The computer not only alters the structure and extent of employment, it also redefines the nature of work. Although the computer releases people from mindless, repetitive and mechanical work, it does not offer any substitute. Work becomes not the fruit of man's labour, but the output of the machine, the means and the end. E. F. Schumacher in his book *Good Work*, points out the three purposes of human work as follows: 'First, to provide necessary and useful goods and services. Second, to enable every one of us to use and thereby perfect our gifts like good stewards. Third, to do so in service to, and in cooperation with, others, so as to liberate ourselves from our inborn egocentricity' (p. 3).

It is against these criteria that we wisely judge the take-over of our work by computers. Modern industrial society, of which computers are the current leading technological expression, has already destroyed the dignity of most forms of work. The computer extends and enhances that process. The goods and services provided by the new technology are seldom, if ever, necessary and their production requires the stimulation of greed, envy and avarice amongst the consumers and producers of those goods. The computer takes away people's skills and only for a small minority does it compensate for that loss of skill not by new skills but by requiring a degree of technical sophistication. Finally, the automated machine takes away our ability to work in service and co-operation with others; it separates us, takes over or interferes with our channels of relationship, pandering to our baser instincts, making our transcendent liberation that much more unlikely. In no sense does the work of machines qualify for the title 'good work', for its effect on the worker or on the person displaced from work is alienating, cutting them off from their roots in humanity.

The impact of computers on work is beginning to be felt, but will increase rapidly in the next few years. Already education is being geared towards a newly defined society, where the notion of unemployment will be replaced by the idea that the full potential labour force will not be required to work. The beginnings of the 'leisure society' can be detected in the tone of official statements, educational programmes and background propaganda. The movement towards continuing and continual education is one such indicator. The drive towards increasing rationalization of industry, the straining for increased productivity and economic competitiveness, make the move towards a 'leisure society' an imperative that will be gained at some cost. The price will be in human and social terms, rather than in cash value and there may be little bargaining in the process of transition. Rada, in the passage quoted above, refers to 'turmoil while the population adjusts', but that assumes that people want to adjust and will, inevitably, adjust. What choice people have to accept or reject a new society, to accept or reject being replaced by a machine at work, is another aspect of the social impact of computer technology, one that we now turn to. The impact on work will be considerable. The international scale of the technology will make the impact considerable on a world-wide scale. The increasing movement towards more flexible and more powerful computer networks, interlinked by information technology, will make the impact dramatic; that drama is, even now, being played around us and we are amongst its participants.

9 CAUGHT IN A MAZE

YOU ARE IN A MAZE OF TWISTY LITTLE PASSAGES, ALL DIFFERENT. The words written up on the screen come from the computer game 'Adventure', which is a fantasy game involving treasure, rescuing princesses, being attacked by giants, dragons and dwarfs and sometimes getting lost in a maze. Different versions of the game have been written for different machines, with the most sophisticated ones being found on large main-frame computers. The maze of passages, all different, is much easier to get out of than the one you can stumble into that says: YOU ARE IN A MAZE OF TWISTY LITTLE PASSAGES, ALL ALIKE. That one requires you to mark each passage somehow to discover whether you have been in it before or not. You need to draw out a map for yourself and hope you won't suddenly be attacked or robbed by some villain, who might be lurking around. In one version of the game there is a maze called WITTS END, which most people cannot escape from, except perhaps by telling the machine that they will commit suicide. In that way they will get reincarnated elsewhere with a subsequent loss of points and the game continues.

Being caught in a maze symbolizes, for me at least, the position we are in with respect to computers generally. We have become caught in a trap of a more perilous kind than the fantasies of 'Adventure'. To start with we have developed, and developed very rapidly, a complex network of a new technology that we do not really understand. The implications of what the new technology is doing are only beginning to be understood and felt by a minority of people. Many more people have feelings of misgivings and fear of the new technology in an instinctive way, and they are rapidly being persuaded that their feelings and fears are misplaced. The problem for most people is how to react to and how to cope with the maze that is enclosing us. Another trap lies in the complexity of computer systems themselves.

Large computer systems have been built that no one understands. Their software will have been developed by a team, whose overall goal would have been well defined, but the different individuals in the team may not necessarily fully comprehend the detailed working of parts of the system other people were putting together. The greater the complexity of the system the more likely will be this situation, with the attendant problem that the different parts of the system will interact in ways no one will be able to predict. Of course, the system will be thoroughly checked and tested, and brought into commission to do exactly what it was designed for, but there will, nevertheless, be interactions that were not explicitly programmed and yet will occur, unpredictably. The system is too complex for anyone to understand.

When the unexpected does occur, providing its effect is discernible, which it may not be (the worst sorts of unexpected interactions are those that alter some other part of the system which will then appear at fault), then another programmer, or even a small team of programmers, will be brought in to sort out the problem. It is unlikely the original programmers will still be around, so the new person or people will have to study the system, or that part of it that has gone awry, and rewrite the necessary codes. They, too, will not fully understand the whole and their corrections may well produce other 'faults' elsewhere and later. Worse than that, the system itself will surely grow and change as the users require extensions of their information processing, additional facilities, etc. As fresh programmers are drawn in to improve and extend the large system so it becomes more incomprehensible and less predictable.

Such systems are around today. They do behave unpredictably, and such behaviour is referred to as 'psychotic'. One example will suffice to illustrate the problem and the dangers of an evolved and over-complex system, namely that used for co-ordinating the defence network in the United States. This system also illustrates the added problem of linking computers together, making for a network of immense complexity whose overall functioning potential is quite unknowable. The US defence network has, on more than one occasion that has been publicly admitted, generated signals whose interpretation, by another part of the network, has been that the country was under attack by the Soviet Union. Such an 'error' was not due to the misinterpretation of radar signals picked up from a flock of birds (that has happened too), but the system itself unpredictably generated a spurious 'under attack' signal. The result was a war alert and missiles with nuclear warheads were sprung into readiness for a counter attack. Luckily the system still needs some final human command but, if that is given on a false basis, then a Doctor Strangelove situation would become reality.

The launching of an attack by such a system without human consultation would, of course, be the most devastating form of HAL scenario one could imagine. HAL was the computer in the science fiction epic *2001*, which decided to take complete command of the space mission because it felt that the astronauts did not have the mission's success at heart. It therefore interpreted their subsequent alarm and counter-measures as evidence for its own viewpoint. HAL became badly 'psychotic' and was eventually dismantled by the only surviving crew member. The HAL scenario is a serious and real problem in computing circles, for those dealing with large systems, and mild versions of it have occurred not infrequently. One computer engineer has said that if his machine answered him back in a completely unprogrammed way he would rip its wires out, but this answering back has already happened in more ways than one.

The large computer system is itself a sort of maze, and one that may not be at all easy to get out of. I have concentrated on describing the problem here because the unpredictable large system is 'out of control'; no one can fully understand it and its functioning may sometimes be other than what is wanted. Even the programmer fights a losing battle with the system, for every change he makes to it, to bring it under his control, alters it in other unpredictable ways so that it always evades him. One trap laid in this maze, then, is the trap of believing that the computer is only a tool that does what you want.

Computer programming is a technical job and programmers have a technical understanding of what is required of them. The aims and functions of a computer system are dictated by its owners and not by the programmers, so the system will be designed to do what the owners want, namely to make their business more efficient. The nature of the business might be commercial, military or governmental; the program will aid that business, but also modify it. The change of technological base alters the nature of the business even though it appears to be merely extending, and making more efficient, current methods. In this way computers revolutionize society by reinforcing the existing structures. This paradox is also part of the trap we are caught in. The computer revolution is changing our lives, but it is doing so by concentrating what we already have, making us more and more dependent on the way things are; extending what we have over ever-increasing scales, wrapping its webbed networks around us. It is also paradoxical that social controllability, which is increased by creating dependence on society's technology, is, as a process, outside social control, in that society does not choose to take that path but has it presented as a *fait accompli*.

When a system is designed and installed in an organization the notion that it does merely what it has been programmed to do becomes a menace, full of hidden dangers. The program is not just a set of instructions but a model of some aspect of the real world. The way the model works, the technical aspects of it, is the realm of the programmer; the output it produces is designed to satisfy the user's needs. However, the user will neither understand how the output is arrived at nor will he probably care; that is a technical matter only. The danger in the system is that the user will, almost inevitably, come to believe in the output and become dependent on it. If an organization pays out large amounts of money for a complex computer system that effectively makes decisions for the user, in that it puts forward 'advice' on future options, then who is going to question it? If the computer says so-and-so and you are not going to believe it, then why spend that money in the first place? The more expensive the system, the more likely users are to believe in it, regardless of their lack of understanding. Ironically, the more complex and expensive the system is, the more likely it is to be unmanageable and less trustworthy.

There are several reasons why a system that claims to produce what it has been designed for should not be trusted. Firstly, there is the basic question of its correct functioning; it may not actually be doing what is required of it. In a simple system this may never be a serious problem, but as we have already discussed, the more complex the system the less clear it may become as to whether the 'true' results are being generated. A computer program for performing scientific calculations that are too complex to be done by hand can be checked in various ways, including being tested against another computer program, independently programmed. If the two give the same results then confidence can be placed in the output, but not necessarily with any more confidence than a belief that the same mistake is unlikely to be made in two independent cases. The results might be false, even if only in a subtle way. Where the system is concerned with human destiny, for example in military or medical areas, then even a subtle error or minor miscalculation could be fatal.

Furthermore faults or failures of components in large systems may not directly affect a particular piece of processing but may insidiously alter the program, data base or limits between processes, within the machine, emerging only later in an incorrect output.

A second reason to mistrust a complex system is purely because it will inevitably be a model of something. A program designed for economic forecasting will construct an electronic model of some part of economic theory and practice. Built into it will be a limited set of assumptions about how economics work and the factors that affect them. However sophisticated the model, it will still be nothing more than a model, incomplete, partial and biased by the assumptions that went to make it. This is true of all programs, whether for engineering design, theoretical physics, medical diagnosis or weather forecasting. The results from such a program will work, appear perfectly credible, and yet be bound by the constrictions in the model and in the way the model has been implemented by the programmer. By playing with the model, different outcomes can be forecast and then interpreted in terms of how the real world will behave. It is this belief that is dangerous, because the computer model is not the real world and never can be. Difficulties arise because the machine appears to be authoritative and the 'model answer' is mistaken for the 'truth'.

One example of the limitations of such modelling is the research that went into the Serpell Report on the future of the

British railways system. The proposals contained in the Report concerned large sections of society, yet the research was based on a model affected by the limiting assumptions on which it was based and the relatively crude computer emulation of those assumptions. Such a report is then intended to be used by government as a basis for future policy, even though the modelling can be shown to be defective or severely limited. The expense and 'authority' of the machine can then be seen to be either dictating policy or being used to justify a policy.

Advice from a machine will always be untrustworthy because it will never take in all the factors that go to make up human experience; dependence on machine advice may result in inhuman action being taken, action taken without responsibility. Weizenbaum has discussed how, in the Vietnam war, computers made 'judgements' as to which villages should be bombed. Decisions taken as a result of such 'judgements' meant that people were killed and maimed and no one was responsible. A machine was. Worse than that, the computers were programmed to lie to the policy decision-makers about what targets had been bombed. The secret bombing of Cambodia went undetected for a while because details of each mission flown by the bombers were falsified by the computer and converted into 'legitimate' (i.e. Vietnamese) targets. Thus the computer rearranges reality and 'creates' history.

The thinking that accompanies computer systems, from the point of view of both the users and the programmers, is such that all problems are seen as having technical solutions, solutions that could be arrived at by using computer techniques. The question is never raised as to whether a particular problem ought to be so treated. Should legal judgements be made by a machine? Is it right to allow a computer to conduct psychotherapy with a patient? Nor does anyone ask whether tackling a problem by using a computer might alter the nature of the problem and the way it is dealt with. Neglect of such matters is another area for concern about the trustworthiness of computer systems; concern about the intentions of those who advocate their use. Those motivations need to be examined and the attitudes inherent in advocating technical solutions understood before any trust is placed in the goods; and yet we find that the machine is trusted, because it is a machine, neutral, cold, objective! The hacker syndrome displays itself all round us. We are caught in that twisty little passage too.

The ethical issue of what computers ought to be used for (about which more in the following chapters) can also arise when they serve as solutions in search of a problem. Investment in a computer means that a use for it is envisaged, but its installation is the start of another twisty passage. Once a computer has been acquired, whether a cheap 'mini' for home use or a large main-frame system for a big organization, its purchase needs justification. Jobs that can be done by the machine are sought rather than seeking the right tool for the job you want to do. In medicine, for example, computers are used for very sophisticated and rare tumour location whilst more pressing medical problems, which do not need complex or glamorous tools to solve them, get set aside. Priorities are altered by computers and hence the machine affects society in unpredictable ways.

When the Pentagon computers 'lied' about the bombing of Cambodia, the machines were merely obeying their ordered sequence of instructions. They 'lied' in that those instructions had been tampered with. The trouble with computer systems is that they are susceptible to fraud and to inaccurate data. Their integrity can be attacked, deliberately, by mistake and by omission. They are also subject to physical damage; all of which makes them insecure and thereby less trustworthy. The trap people fall into is in believing them safe.

Computer security is a difficult and involved matter and one concerned not just with physical protection, prevention of misuse, crime and illegal access but also with the integrity of information put into the machine. A business forecasting program will not be of much use, for example, if the data it is supplied with is inaccurate. Planning decisions based on an analysis of census data will be worthless if there are errors in the information fed into the machine. Such errors can occur at any point in data collection: incorrect completion of the original form, the mis-coding of that information, input errors when the data is fed into the machine, and so on. The questions that have not been asked may also have a relevance to the reliability of the forecasting program. The forecast will only be as good as its model as well as its data and it is often the unforeseen factors that make reality so different from people's expectations of what will happen. Of course all these problems arise without computers, so why should the machine make any difference?

The computer will be used when the scale of a situation warrants it. There is little point in analysing data for very individualistic decision-making, for example on whether to go to the theatre tonight or not, because although the number of factors involved may be considerable, such decision-making involves unquantifiable and subjective factors. In trying to forecast the economic future of a business, however, a computer might well be employed, because the problem seems too large. In the past, people coped with such situations reasonably enough. Even the Second World War was conducted without computer 'advice', but the presence of computers seems to demand their use. In analysing the factors that affect the business's future, gross simplification may be made in order to handle the problem technically. So, whereas in the past the boss knew his employees and their personal histories, problems, strengths and weaknesses, and used that qualitative information, however unconsciously, in making decisions, the same decision-making today ignores all but the simplified and quantified factors. The use of the computer also seems to convey a feeling of objectivity to an analysis, giving it the appearance of greater reliability, but the quality of such decision-making may well be inferior, even if proved to be 'economically' superior. The inhuman machine leads to inhuman decision-making. The unquantifiable factors are squeezed out and no longer seem to matter. Furthermore, when the problem is very large, such as in governing a country, then it appears attractive to tackle the problem by using vast amounts of data, as if bare facts themselves contain the solution to circumstances which actually require wisdom, rather than hard knowledge, to sort out. Government and commerce have become technical, too.

The reliability of information stored in computers becomes acutely important when the data concerns people's personal details, their medical, social, employment and financial records, their political and religious affiliations, marital status and so forth. Such data (and much other information) is confidential, so that not only the reliability but also the security of computer systems must be safeguarded. Such information must be protected against being altered by mistake, or by design, as well as protected from unauthorized access. Like all computer data it needs physical protection from fire, water, magnetic damage and even sabotage. Storage environments must be carefully controlled and monitored and, where the data or programs are especially valuable, separate copies must be stored elsewhere for double security. Computer security is now big business and the question of access to and privacy for personal information stored on computers has become a lively public issue.

Access to confidential files can be protected by use of suitable sets of passwords and codes, known only to those who have a right of access. Built into the computer system can be a number of such safeguards and double checks. Computer recognition of fingerprints or voice patterns would provide perhaps the clearest means of ensuring that only valid users had access to private files. Of course, no system is totally secure and where money or other gain is involved someone will always find a way of breaking the system. In this way computers have found themselves the focal centres of industrial espionage, embezzlement and fraud. The people with the best means of abusing, for their own purposes, any computer system are the programmers and computer operators and it is amongst them that a new breed of criminal has arisen, albeit on a small scale.

Two techniques demonstrate how fraud can be practised on computer systems. The first is called the Salami technique as it involves embezzling small slices of money over a long period of time. An account is opened by the embezzler who has access to, say, a banking accounts system. He arranges for the money, fictional money in a sense, thrown away in rounding down uneven sums in accounting, to be transferred to his special account. So, when someone's interest is being calculated and it comes to £17.853, the 0.3 of a penny is paid to the fraud and not discarded. He is not stealing money from anyone (except possibly the bank) and his account grows in thin slices to quite considerable sums. More insidious, and more difficult to detect is the technique known as the logic bomb. A program is written with this sort of section in it:

line 1565   WHEN some condition applies pay x thousand pounds into

account number 12345. OTHERWISE go to line 1567
line 1566   DELETE line numbers 1565 and 1566

When the embezzler is ready, the condition he has specified can be input to the system and a large amount is paid to him and the evidence in the program self-destroyed. Such a crime is very hard to detect, apart from the sudden loss of considerable sums of money. Computer crime is often on a large scale, sometimes involving frauds of millions of pounds, and the criminals quite frequently get away with it, because commercial firms do not want to make public the fact that their system is not foolproof. Frequently the embezzler is helped to find a better job in another company, accompanied by glowing references, so that he can do the same thing elsewhere!

Computer systems, their programs and their data, are insecure things in that they concentrate information, which is today's currency. More and more organizations have put more and more of their functions into computers and in this way have become almost totally reliant on the machine and also more insecure at the same time. Damage to the machine or to its software and data could cripple a firm or bring chaos to a public agency. Sabotage to a banking computer centre could result in financial bedlam; disruption to the international airline booking system computer network would result in a traveller's nightmare. Increasingly, large computer systems operators are becoming very security-conscious: personnel are carefully vetted; physical movements in and around computer installations are monitored and regulated. Staff may be required to carry identification discs which open doors, but which also supply information as to who is where. The computer system knows the location of all its human components. You could not throw your disc out of a window to an accomplice because the door would not open twice to what would appear to be the same person trying to come through it in the same direction. The high security buildings of the new society will be the computer centres, and such places are already becoming self-protective. Another trap found in our maze is the belief that we could rip the wires out of the machine if it turned out to be a beast. It could fight back. Just imagine the Hopkins Beast, seeking out its own electricity supply, but armed in order to prevent anyone stopping it in its single-minded mission. Extend such a picture to a computer with its own electrical generating plant, linked into a network so that it can ensure sufficient supplies to keep itself running and also armed to prevent anyone switching it off. It would be simple to install, a trivial piece of software and hardware to implement. Its result would be terrifying. The HAL scenario is not just science fiction.

A computer-based society becomes a fragile society, easily disrupted, held in the grip of a small technical élite who would have enormous potential power. The controllers and operators of the communications channels could exert massive political and social pressure. The technology concentrates power, although it appears to decentralize it. Spreading the computer network into every house, just as television has spread, appears to be bringing the power of computer and information systems to every corner of society. What it in fact does is to tighten the grip of a few on the many. More people become dependent for their entertainment, their news and information, even their financial arrangements and housekeeping facilities on a small group of people who control and manipulate the system for their own ends. The greater our technological dependence becomes (the more 'freedom' technology gives us), the more fragile does society become.

Technological dependence makes a society essentially unstable. It means that communities of people come to rely, for their needs (their food, work and social interactions), on organizations beyond the horizon of their own community. The technological infrastructure of a technologically based society removes functions from local to regional, national or even international levels. Food is not grown by the local community but is provided by an agricultural industry backed up by a complex food processing and distribution scheme that itself depends on other industries, such as the petro-chemical industry, which themselves are unstable and subject to many other interrelated concerns. Each link in these technological and economic chains is weak, and the more complex the system becomes the weaker the whole chain becomes. A stable society can provide for its own needs on a local scale and would only look further for luxuries. An unstable technological society regards even luxuries as essential, because to produce them may be profitable, economic progress being the sole criterion for judging success. However, any system that must grow to progress is inherently unstable and economies that require continued expansion are inevitably fragile and inevitably technologically based.

The instability of a technologically dependent society is also shown when restrictions have to be imposed on the rights of its citizens. The high-security computer installation, like the nuclear power station, reduces the citizen's rights. The need to protect society's high technology comes at the expense of restricting what citizens may do or where they may be allowed to go. With soft computer technology the loss of rights comes primarily in the form of loss of privacy of information and the difficulty of finding out what information is held by whom, for what purpose, on whom. Countries themselves are not immune. Spy satellites look down on the neutral as well as on the hostile. We are all, globally, overlooked, so that whatever is done, anywhere, is done in public. At the time of writing the Third World countries have just persuaded the industrialized nations to guarantee them the right to inspect all data concerning their own territory taken from remote sensing satellites. The United Kingdom opposed such a move; the USA, USSR, France and Japan (who operate the satellites) said nothing on the matter at all. This is not just a sign of the times but a reflection of the attitude of those who have the technology; they want to retain its control and its power and are even reluctant to share the information gained with those to whom it applies.

An information-based society stores vast quantities of data and the spread of computer-based information systems has generated the demand for ever increasing numbers of files. Information is kept about individuals' financial dealings, their health records and records on social security, local authority dealings, tax, credit, hire purchase, car licensing, education, library use, employment details, police record ... the list is almost endless. There are records of whose existence the people concerned have no idea, let alone what the records say. People have no right of access to what is stored about them, to see whether it is correct, complete, up to date, or even necessary. In several countries new laws have been brought into effect to protect people's privacy and permit them access to some of the files concerning them, but in Britain governments have deferred the issue again and again. Even when legislation exists and people can inspect and validate information kept about them, it is not clear whether they see every file or even know that some files exist. Ignorance puts people in a subservient position.

As with all data, personal information may be stored in an incomplete or incorrect form. Many people, for example, have experienced quite long delays in getting a computerized system to alter their address when they have moved. That, of course, is just bad management, but when systems get very large that sort of inefficiency is more liable to occur and any individual problem the more difficult to sort out. Institutions have always kept files and details about people's individual lives but, until recently, records have not been centralized, the scale of record-keeping has been local and reasonably manageable. An old-fashioned filing system may be less efficient from the standpoint of the manager wanting to look at a particular file than is a computer-based one (although that is not always the case), but from the viewpoint of the person whose file it is, the old system was more accessible, easier to get checked and amended. It was also more secure. Of course, a file in a metal filing cabinet can be stolen, if someone is desperate to get it, and it can easily be mislaid or put in the wrong place, but under normal circumstances it is not likely that an unauthorized person could easily obtain access to it. With computerized files this is not the case.

The real issue concerning privacy and computerized files is that as networked systems grow, as more computers 'talk' to other computers, then privacy of files becomes increasingly difficult to maintain, data is used impersonally and no one takes responsibility. As computers become connected into national-scale networks, so will it become feasible for almost anyone to gain access to large data banks. In the United States, university students found a way of breaking into such systems so that not only could they gain access to files, but were also able to delete them or alter them. That example was only one case amongst many, but was described by Stanford Research Institute as an example of 'the most serious computer security problem'. Even knowledge of such a problem raises legal and ethical issues. Would manufacturers of computers be liable for their vulnerability? Would a research institute be liable to notify users who might be affected? Should knowledge of such techniques be shared or kept secret?

Consider a finance company being asked to provide a loan. Of course, it is perfectly correct that the company should check the financial status of the applicant, and his or her ability to repay the loan, but even relatively easy access to other sources of information, such as health or police records, could influence, quite unfairly, a decision about granting that loan. Refusal to offer the loan would not be based on the information given, presumably in all honesty, by the applicant. Similarly applicants for a job could be 'investigated' by examining records about their life, unknown to them and therefore not answerable to by them. This would be bad enough if the records were accurate, but would be grossly unjust if the records were misleading or false. Credit companies have been known to refuse credit to someone who lives in a 'high risk' area. Despite someone's own financial integrity, if the neighbours have a bad credit rating, his or hers may be marked bad by implication. Then that person may apply for a job, for example as a cashier in a shop, and the employer surreptitiously checks his or her credit rating, not wanting a potential embezzler. By obtaining information that is misleading an error of judgement can be made, against which there is no safeguard.

It is so easy to store information in a computer but so impersonal that other sorts of problem can arise. Consider a police file. Keeping computer records on criminals, suspects, and people 'known to the police' (who might be doctors and lawyers, as well as rogues), rather than written records, makes for an impersonal system with subsequently inhumane consequences. When a policeman notices something suspicious, or notes some unusual behaviour, even when he takes down the names of people in a club raided for drugs, he is personally responsible for his records and can use them as an *aide mémoire* to recall the event to which they refer. The same information in a computer can be 'read' by many other officers, can be treated as 'objective facts' and not associated with a more complex remembered reality. A person's name can be filed in a police computer without their knowledge and without their having committed an offence or even being suspected of one. A witness to an accident, an innocent bystander in a drugs raid, could both end up 'known to the police'. A colleague of mine, who has professional associations with the probation service, was surprised to be told he was filed in the local police computer.

Even when the record is straight, if access to it can be made irregularly, then that information can be abused.

The ability to alter or erase other people's files could cause not just an increase in computer crime, but also a whole range of business, political or personal abuses. A form of computer game could then be played by youngsters with a networked terminal, putting fortunes into poor people's accounts and giving the wealthy huge overdrafts! Teachers could suddenly find themselves with detailed criminal records, or discover they have died of lung cancer! Insurance frauds, already popular as one form of computer crime, can be practised most effectively if records can be altered and so too could blackmail. Perhaps the most sinister form of using networks of computer data files, however, is to monitor people's behaviour for some form of 'intelligence' work.

There is a great deal known about many, many people and much of that information is stored in computer-accessible data banks. Someone assembling that information could piece together a surprisingly detailed picture of any individual and his or her life. Just access to their bank file would reveal a great deal. Apart from general financial transactions, details about standing orders would reveal what organizations, religious groups, political parties, clubs and so forth a person belonged to. If someone belonged to a book or record club their taste in reading and music could be discovered. Their reading could also be monitored via a library system. Computerized shopping, paid for by an EFT card, would enable someone's every purchase to be monitored. Insurance company files would give details of household contents and motor vehicles in someone's possession; even how accident prone they were. Health, social security and education files would give plenty of details about a person and his or her family. In the fully electronic home, computer centred, all manner of private information could be accessible. Privacy would be reduced to almost nothing. Electronic cash registers have already been used to monitor the efficiency of the cashiers and every piece of chip-based technology is capable of a similar monitoring function. A cable television system, allowing two-way communication between home or office and central information and entertainment networks, provides the means whereby continuous monitoring of who is seeing what and when could be carried out. George

Orwell's prediction in *1984* of Big Brother watching you, was not far wrong. Instead of being watched by an all-seeing eye, we can be monitored just as effectively as we use any part of an electronic network or two-way television and computer system. Such technology is almost exactly the mechanism of *1984*'s Big Brother. It is a technology for control.

The monitoring of telephone calls, something that has been done for decades, also becomes so much easier with chip-based devices. For some years, international telex and telephone calls have been systematically monitored; now public agencies are developing speech recognition programs that will enable such procedures to be employed on a far wider scale. The listening machine deprives people even of the privacy of a conversation, admittedly a conversation via a technological link. In *2001* HAL could even lip-read!

There is no need to stop at telephone calls. Already experiments have been conducted on monitoring the whereabouts of people wearing an electronic 'bleeper'. People convicted of less serious crimes can be offered an alternative to prison by having a ring sealed round their ankle which contains such a transmitting device, whose signal is detected and analysed by a network of small computers. There would be no technical reason to prevent such a scheme being extended to monitoring the whereabouts of every motor vehicle or even of all people in a society. The technology is able to provide that degree of social control; it can make privacy a historical concept.

In these and other ways, interlinked computer systems provide a ready means for groups to investigate and monitor the private lives of people they want to control for one reason or another. Anything performed via a cable, satellite or telephone link, any information passed via a terminal, is subject to being monitored. The fantasies of science fiction writers in this respect are being fulfilled with remarkable rapidity. What can be monitored can be controlled. By creating greater dependence on machines and machine-based communications channels, those who generate the systems gain greater control. Satellite television for example spreads the control of images, 'news', opinion, to a greater population. Empires today are won by those who control the controlling technology. This maze has passages all alike.

Many personal choices are dictated by the technology accessible to people. A way of life can be increasingly determined by what is available rather than by what people decide for themselves. Most technology, and especially the new technology, is accompanied by the most sophisticated advertising and propaganda, so it becomes increasingly difficult to separate out what a person would really like from the background of imperialistic technology. Information technology as well, in its soft, more ephemeral way, affects choice. What information there is and the way it is manipulated and controlled, dictates people's choice very strongly. The notion of 'divide and rule' is exactly how technologies are used, especially information technology. The telephone gives people the 'freedom' to talk to anyone connected to the system, but at the expense of reducing human interaction to one of disembodied voices. Social control is gained by dividing people from one another by interfacing them via technologies, technologies that serve, not the people, but those who control them.

In this way traditional communities are broken up and people scattered. The technological society depends on depriving people of their simple needs and making them dependent on technologically produced essentials and artificial needs.

This imperialism extends world-wide, for that is where the network of technology extends. Bringing educational TV to the villages of India or Africa sounds enterprising enough, but in reality it is a means of imposing on people, quite unprepared for it, images and concepts that derive from another culture. It matters not what is shown via such technology, nor how much involvement the 'local' people have in its programming. The device itself brings a cultural package inseparable from the contents. The global village McLuhan discussed is a concept that springs from a high-technology society. As that society spreads across the globe, the village earth becomes unified as a high-technology community; local characteristics, people's real needs and their ways of self expression become subsumed to an impersonal, bland and soulless machine-oriented outlook.

Within the developed, sophisticated countries, education (including the acceptance and adoption of new technologies) can also be an instrument of social control. The notion of education for leisure really means conditioning people to accept the machine replacement of human jobs. Rada, in the quotation presented in the last chapter, wrote 'while the population tries to adjust to ...', implying that electronic technology itself forces people to accept it, and people must therefore make that adjustment, however radical or dehumanizing the adjustment may be. Technological progress is always described as inevitable, unstoppable. Its power to control, to dominate whole populations is seldom challenged.

So much for democracy then! If people's lives are governed by the unelected controllers of technology, the freedoms granted by democratic vote are totally undermined. If governments are all helpless in the face of advancing technology, then however they are elected matters only in terms of detail and style, because their power is notional and subject to the will of the technocrats. Who voted for the telephone, for television, for the microprocessor? Who chose to lose their jobs to a machine? Does the freedom given, to push one button on the TV set or another, compensate for the fact that the images are planted there by people who have their interest at heart and not yours? Who chose to make computer games games of violence: space invaders, star *wars*, etc.? Is the notion of democracy itself 'sold' as a technological concept by those whose technologies divide and rule? Who supplies democracy, and to whom are they answerable?

Such questions need consideration, just as do those we should all ask with respect to information stored about us. Who wants it, for what reason? It would be easy to speculate about some vast conspiracy, designed to ensnare us all in the hands of the industrial/military complex. The replacement of human beings by machines in the processes of production, and the redundancy of human beings in the processes of social organization look suspiciously like villainous social engineering. I am not going to speculate along those lines, however, for what looks like a conspiracy is, I suspect, a game gone wrong. The twisty little passages of a computer network have engulfed us. The game has outgrown itself and has placed us at Witts End, not knowing where we are or where we can go to. The only question left is whether we can escape by switching off the machine that engendered our dilemma or whether we are caught in a maze of twisty little passages of our own making.

10 FORBIDDEN FRUIT

The development of technologies is always motivated, at least in part, by the desire to control nature and to overcome the restraints nature places on people. The common belief of the past two to three hundred years is that the 'scientific method' is the most productive means man has discovered with which to conquer nature and, in the twentieth century, the application of science to an ever increasing variety of problems has led us to the situation where the major outstanding questions being faced are those concerning 'life' and 'mind'. The recent advent of the science and technology of genetic engineering has opened up questions about the 'creation of life' in the laboratory and of the alteration of life forms by the manipulative scientist. Part of the methodology and thinking behind such work is that of classical reductionism, namely that by taking something to pieces and putting it together again a complete understanding of the thing will be gained. In fact such an approach is only a parody of understanding, but it is seen most starkly in those scientists who are investigating life and the equally nebulous phenomenon of mind.

The question of 'mind' or 'intelligence' is often approached pragmatically, using the following argument: if a system can be built that displays desired characteristics then such a system possesses the properties that are required to produce such characteristics. If a machine can mimic a human function then it can be said to behave, at least partially, in a human way. This behaviourist approach is found widely in computer circles and is applied by reducing human functions to their quantitative elements, ignoring both the complexity of the interaction of the parts of the whole person and the existence of non-quantifiable and higher levels of the human condition. The fallacy in the argument was poignantly illustrated in the classic children's story of 'The Emperor's Nightingale', where the imitation of the real thing, however sophisticated, could never match the genuine beauty of the living thing being parodied.

The aim of late twentieth-century science and technology is the complete conquest of nature, manifest in a totally controlled artificial environment. The supposed final frontiers are even now being faced in the genetics engineering research institutions and the high-technology computer laboratories. In the one place the very processes of life itself are being sought and manipulated, in the other, means for complete 'intellectual' control of this artificial world are being developed. Where the geneticists work from the bottom up, trying to fit the most elementary pieces together, to build whole living things from their parts, the computer researchers work from the top down, trying to mimic human functions of 'mind'. The cross-connections between the two fields are many. Both, for example, deal with information. In computing, 'intelligence' is treated as the capacity to process and analyse information and in genetics the DNA molecule, the biochemical basis of the genetic code, is regarded as an information system. Both areas work towards effects; creating an organism that displays certain properties, producing a system that 'thinks'. Both areas of research also assume that life is purely the working interaction of the parts of an organism and that mind is nothing other than the electro-chemical operation of an organic computer. Neither science recognizes any transcendent faculties in man.

Artificial intelligence and new species, both created by science and technology, are the aims of such developments. The technologies themselves are attempting to play God by redefining nature in their own terms, by trying to manipulate the processes of life and mind and by attempting to control completely their own creations. Such an aspiration was foretold in the book of Genesis, when God forbade Adam and Eve to eat of the tree of knowledge, lest they become like gods. Our science has now reached such extremes in manipulating nature that our scientists and technologists have more than dared, they have already picked the forbidden fruits. The irony of the situation, however, is seen in the fruits of their work, which produce not an edifying view of the dignity of man but an image of such mediocrity that it is not surprising that the comparison can then be drawn between man and machine.

'Artificial Intelligence' has been described as 'how to make computers smarter' (B. Raphael) at a simplistic but realistic level and more grandiosely as 'the development of a systematic theory of intellectual processes' (Michie). Margaret Boden chooses Minsky's definition as the least contentious: 'artificial intelligence is the science of making machines do things that would require intelligence if done by men', which is just one version of the behaviourist argument. Her own meaning of the term covers 'all machine research that is somehow relevant to human knowledge and psychology'. The connection between psychology and machine intelligence is not surprising, because it is from psychology that we have come to define (and limit) what is meant by human intelligence and such a conception, built into machines, is being used as feedback for exploring a variety of psychological models.

Much of the research work into machine intelligence is closely linked with work in psychology. Attempts at finding general theories of problem solving and of understanding the basis of natural language are perhaps the main general areas for seeking understanding. However, it seems to me that the whole approach is based on a very limited view of the nature of intelligence and of human beings. It is only necessary to compare Homer's view, that intelligence is a gift of grace, with that of a modern psychologist, 'intelligence is what the intelligence test measures', to see the modern limitation of outlook. The aims of such work are also very grandiose. Both these points are displayed in the statement by Professor John McCarthy, of Stanford University: 'The only reason we have not yet succeeded in formalizing every aspect of the real world is that we have been lacking a sufficiently powerful logical calculus'. The desire to encompass all possible understanding is certainly grandiose, and naïvely simplistic, but the notion that the real world can be 'formalized' by a 'calculus' is part of the general fallacy widely found in the sciences. Because the behaviour of some physical phenomena can be approximated by mathematical expressions it is ridiculously assumed that the whole real world is underlain by one powerful formula; whereas the world is complex and unique beyond description.

Of course, treating artificial intelligence as a field in which certain human functions are simulated or surpassed has powerful and maybe useful results. Clearly, computers can process information of some kinds much more rapidly and accurately than can people, but such operations cannot validly be described as intelligence, even when the program continues by evaluating its own computations according to some present criteria. Intelligent thought should at least be regarded as the determination of the requirements of a situation in the light of individual perceptions, education, environmental and cultural factors, indeed the whole range of personal experience and setting that makes people other than 'mere machines'. Until computers have developed to the point where they are like that, the word 'intelligent' should not really be applied to them.

Of course, sophisticated programs have been developed that enable machines to 'learn' and even to 'originate' output. Programs can simulate language and appear to 'converse' with people. An example of such a conversation comes from K. M. Colby's program. (Machine output in capitals)

I hate you, you stupid machine.
WHAT DON'T YOU LIKE ABOUT ME?
You have no feelings.
HOW DO YOU MEAN?
I mean you cannot experience what I experience because you are just a machine.
TELL ME MORE ABOUT SUCH FEELINGS.
We are not communicating.
I AM TRYING MY BEST TO COMMUNICATE WITH YOU.
Are you really?
HOW DO YOU SEE IT?
I think you are all goofed up.

However, it is wrong to consider such programs as doing anything more than manipulating symbols according to some particular theory. Psychologists and computer scientists will then argue that that is just what humans do, but on a more complex basis; such an outlook ignores the complex of individual factors that each person brings to each situation. In contrast each machine has only its program, which effectively never changes. But even when the time comes when machines can modify their own programs according to both their own perceptions (via mechanical limbs, TV eyes and so on) and their own experience, they will still not have human intelligence, they will be intelligent machines.

This sort of speculation, however, is itself a reflection of the way in which artificial intelligence research is engaged in a redefinition of the world that goes against all the values that were set up as a standard in Chapter 1. Machine intelligence, which we must always distinguish from human intelligence as being something different, alien, is not a gift of grace, nor is it associated with the human ability to discern right from wrong and to perceive things spiritual. The computer may have a brain but will never have a heart. Machine intelligence, when and if it comes about, will really be machine reason.

The reasonable and reasoning machine may well appear to simulate many features that human beings admire and seek to attain themselves, but there is a danger in that, which has been highlighted by Weizenbaum. He has stated that it would be unethical to assign to a machine a job that should be conducted by a human being because the job relates to the human condition. Professor McCarthy once asked, 'What do judges know that we cannot tell a computer?' The answer at one level (in terms of pure reason) is 'nothing', but at another level (that of the human condition) the answer is overwhelmingly 'everything'. However smart the reasoning machine may become it will never be a human being and its experience will always relate to its machine condition.

Margaret Boden believes that artificial intelligence will 'counteract the subtly dehumanizing influence of natural science . . . by showing . . . how it is possible for psychological beings to be grounded in a material world and yet be properly distinguished from "mere matter"'. It can do so, she argues, by reconciling the mechanistic descriptions of the sciences with the subjective experience of human beings. My response to such a notion is again based on the artificiality of machine intelligence; to use the machine as a guide to how to be human both denies the richness of mankind's experience of humanity and our collected wisdom and lowers our view of what it means to be a person by reflecting ourselves in a machine mirror. Margaret Boden's arguments leave out any mention of a spiritual dimension to man. In modern psychology such dimensions are at best reduced, along with other qualities, to nothing more than some particular psychological state. The psychology that is linked with computers is also part of reductionist science.

Research in artificial intelligence continues apace. Work is reported in a number of areas but, plainly, pattern recognition, especially speech recognition, is one important area. Language analysis and translation provide a field of both practical and theoretical scope for research as does the whole area of expert systems and automated inquiry systems. Much effort is being put into advanced forms of robotics, with machines being designed to 'learn' and to 'experience' by analysing what they can 'sense' via television eyes, sensitized limbs and so on. General-purpose robots, that can be taught and commanded to do any task required, would clearly be more useful than machines dedicated to one particular sort of function. Even new forms of electronics are being proposed, which operate rather more like biological neurones than telegraph wires. Such a development could have a startling impact on future trends in the micro-electronic industry and in the research towards the intelligent machine.

New generations of computers are now being designed that will not only replace present-day machines but also make them look like museum pieces. The so-called fifth generation machines, that are currently being designed, will be based on the most advanced techniques of artificial intelligence. The aim of their builders is to produce ultra-sophisticated machines that can 'talk' freely with people, interpret natural language to avoid the present-day problems of programming, and then be able to perform the functions their users want. Alongside this research is a more general awareness in computer circles of making machines increasingly 'user friendly'; that is enabling man/machine interaction to be as easy and 'natural' as possible. In 1958 Herbert Simon and Allen Newell, of Carnegie-Mellon University, Pittsburgh, claimed: 'There are now in the world machines that think, that learn and that create. Moreover, their ability to do these things is going to increase rapidly until in the visible future the range of problems they can handle will be coextensive with the range to which the human mind has been applied'.

Such a statement, it could be argued, is little more than a propaganda exercise and it could just as easily have been stated in 1983. Perhaps that is a reflection of what little progress has been made towards developing a machine that 'thinks' in the last twenty-five years, but the hope expressed certainly matches the ambitions of the 'generation five' machine designers. Just as the genetic engineers are aiming to produce new species, so the artificial intelligence researchers are aiming at creating the very intelligent machine.

The Ultra-Intelligent Machine (UIM) was first postulated by Jack Good, who worked with Michie under Alan Turing on the Colossus project at Bletchley Park. The UIM is merely an extension of the idea of a machine as intelligent as a human being. If such a machine could be built, argued Good, then with a little more effort a computer more intelligent than human beings could be developed. The UIM, by definition, would be able to perform any intellectual activity at least marginally better than a person, but, of course, when such a machine has been built it will be able to design even more intelligent machines and the process will escalate until man will live 'in the interstices of uncomprehended, incredibly intelligent electronic organisms, like fleas on the backs of dogs', as Donald Michie puts it.

At this point it is worth returning briefly to the subject of the nature of intelligence. Christopher Evans gives as a definition: the ability of a system to adjust appropriately to a changing world; and he makes this definition more specific by examining six factors that go to make up this view of intelligence. These are the ability to sense or gather information about the outside world, the capacity to store that information, speed of processing data, together with flexibility, efficiency and range of inbuilt software. Such a description of intelligence assumes that software is essentially a 'written' code built into a biochemical organism, much as a program is 'placed' in a computer. This intelligence is single-valued and can be scaled, for example, over a range where rocks have an IQ of 0, fish 100,000 and people 1,000,000. On such a scale Evans places computers at an IQ of around 3,000, above the tapeworm but below the earwig! However, he claims computers will *evolve* very rapidly up the scale as they do not have to be burdened with interlocking suites of programs to enable them to move, feed, repair themselves or enjoy food, drink and other sensory thrills, such as basking in the sun and making love. Surely, one point about human intelligence is that it encompasses all those things. Evans wants to separate out *intelligence* from 'psycho-motor co-ordination' and the 'major task of keeping a complex body alive and active', so he is really referring, not to intelligence, but to the ability of organisms to reason. Evans's argument is another example of defining a significant human quality in terms that enable computers to be endowed with that quality. The difference between a person and an earwig, in terms of intelligence, is not our superiority in adjusting to a changing world but in seeing a wide range of meaning in the events of our lives. If we squeeze out the comprehension of meaning from the notion of intelligence then we should also remove the ideas of intuition, imagination, creativity (except in a very limited form), the poetic, the feminine and the mystical. Such a degraded view of intelligence, derived by mirroring man in the technology of computers, is tantamount to discounting everything that our culture and history has valued. The world is redefined in a less than human way.

In a similar way other qualities also get distorted or redefined. One such quality is that of enchantment, of bewitching, beguiling and making magic. Professor Alan Newell said in a lecture:

the little boxes that make out your income tax for you—the brakes that know how to stop on wet pavements . . . instruments that can converse with their users . . . bridges that watch out for the safety of those who cross them . . . street lights that care about those who stand under them, who know the way so no one need get lost. In short, computer technology offers the possibility of incorporating intelligent behaviour in all the nooks and crannies of our world. With it we can build an enchanted land.

By 'enchantment' here Newell means technically sophisticated, and certainly not magic (except in the sense of tricky illusion). This quotation illustrates the confusion between what Heinz Zemenek calls type No. 1 and type No. 2 worlds. World type No. 1 is the real world, the human world we all live in. World No. 2 is the formalized, logical world of scientific description. It is a theoretical world based on abstractions, equations, sequences of symbols and it is often in hopeless contrast to the real world we know and live in. The trouble with computers, which operate within type 2 formalism, is the ease with which we can anthropomorphize them, give them human, type No. 1 qualities they do not possess; Newell illustrates this tendency in the passage above. Such assignments of type No. 1 qualities on to a type No. 2 object lead to many of the confusions shown about computers, not least of which is the professional discussion of machine intelligence in terms of human thought.

The question of volition and purpose also creeps into this confusion. Terms such as 'know', 'watch out for' and 'care', all from the passage above, are used in the human sense. To 'know' something is different from 'having knowledge stored' in a system. To know assumes consciousness and self awareness (to some extent) and certainly to care assumes a whole range of human attributes including love. To discuss street lights as 'caring' is not only to misapply a human term to a technical device, to confuse world type 2 with type 1, but is also to misapply a comparison between a machine and a person to the detriment of the person. Caring involves not just 'intelligence' but also the human emotions, including the desire to relate to and help others. There is a difference between wanting to do something and being designed to do something. A vacuum cleaner would not 'want' to clean the floor, even if it was fully automated, and cleaned up whenever the floor got dirty or whenever commanded to do so. Making the machine respond to the question, 'Why did you do that?', by having it answer, 'Because I wanted to', does not mean the machine has a will or a self-directed purpose, merely that it has been made 'user friendly'.

It has been suggested that the more intelligent computers will need to have some form of myth or religion built into them to enable them to self-direct their own purpose in a suitably moral way. Such a suggestion assumes that myths and religions are purely 'psychological necessities', rather than truths about reality; an attitude to be expected from a technological world view that imagines ultra-intelligent computers that will compete with and excel all human functions. The idea goes back to that expressed in Isaac Asimov's 'I Robot' stories and his well known 'laws of Robotics'. These state that a robot must not harm, or through inactivity allow to come to harm, a human being; that a robot must obey all commands given to it by a human being except when these conflict with the first law and a robot must preserve itself at all times unless by doing so it contradicts the first two laws. The idealism of these laws contrasts starkly with the writings and predictions of workers in artificial intelligence today.

Already various ethical codes and religious doctrines have been programmed into computers so that they can give suitable 'advice' to people who want help within a particular tradition. That is something slightly different, but the extension of that idea is the notion of a 'Hindu' or a 'Christian' computer that could offer pastoral counselling, preach sermons and act as a 'spiritual' guide. 'Super computers', it is projected, will take over not just religion, but politics, economics, law, work and leisure, as well as medicine, education, our personal relationships and even provide us with computerized sex. The pornographic computer does not bear thinking about, but neither does the proposal, made in earnest, that future computers will so reduce our need to use our brains that we will need to take up mental jogging, using programs especially designed to exercise the mind. It seems to me that before computers have religious or ethical codes built into them, the computer scientists might adopt some of their own, to direct their purposes in a suitably moral way, rather than propagate wild fantasies.

The link between artificial intelligence and psychology stems from their commonly shared view of man. This has been made quite explicit by several of the leading figures in this area of research. For example the psychologist George Miller wrote: 'Many psychologists have come to take for granted in recent years ... that men and computers are merely two different species of a more abstract genus called "information processing systems".' Colby, Watt and Gilbert, reviewing the role of computer programs for psychotherapy, said: 'A human therapist can be viewed as an information processor and decision maker with a set of rules which are clearly linked to short range and long range goals'. Such attitudes then lead to notions of machines being able to 'treat' ten times the number of patients that can be handled now, and so defects in present-day psychotherapy management become 'solved' by the computer. Other alternatives are not considered because the machine can 'solve' the problem. But the 'solution' is a technical one and the real human problem underlying the needs of the patients is neither analysed nor even discussed. The problem is seen merely as one of 'numbers', which is not surprising when people are reclassified in an inhuman way. Consider the statement by the computer scientist Herbert A. Simon in his book *The Sciences of the Artificial*:

An ant, viewed as a behaving system, is quite simple. The apparent complexity of the environment in which it finds itself . . . the truth or falsity of [this] hypothesis should be independent of whether ants, viewed more microscopically, are simple or complex systems. At the level of cells or molecules, ants are demonstrably complex; but these microscopic details of the inner environment may be largely irrelevant to the ant's behaviour in relation to the outer environment. That is why an automaton, though completely different at the microscopic level, might nevertheless simulate the ant's gross behaviour . . .
I should like to explore this hypothesis, but with the word 'man' substituted for 'ant'. *A man, viewed as a behaving system, is quite simple. The apparent complexity of his behaviour over time is largely a reflection of the complexity of the environment in which he finds himself* . . . I myself believe that this hypothesis holds even for the whole man. (pp. 24–5)

Simon is not unaware of the problem of the redefinition of man in terms of the machine. In an article entitled 'What Computers Mean for Man and Society', he entitles a whole section 'Man's view of man', and questions whether man's dignity and sense of worth (he does not mention any other human qualities) depend on man's unique position in nature. In practice, though, Simon does not answer his own questions except to reassert his own ideology. He writes:

The definition of man's uniqueness has always formed the kernel of his cosmological and ethical systems. With Copernicus and Galileo, he ceased to be the species located at the centre of the universe, attended by the sun and stars. With Darwin, he ceased to be the species created and specially endowed by God with soul and reason. With Freud, he ceased to be the species whose behaviour was—potentially— governable by rational mind. As we begin to produce mechanisms that think and learn, he has ceased to be the species uniquely capable of complex, intelligent manipulation of his environment.

Simon answers his question 'what is man?' by repeating his own view that man is the species that has now learned that his mind is 'explainable in terms of simple mechanisms'. Such a bleak outlook on human nature and the human interactions of life is hard to comprehend. There is no room for love or beauty or friendship, no place for shared experience, prayer or suffering, pity, grief or caring. Man thus reduced to simple mechanisms should be redefined as a machine. The only trouble lies with the term 'machine'.

If the term machine has connotations of rigidity, simplicity and repetitive behaviour, argues Simon, then such a term would mis-describe the computer. He continues: 'We must either get rid of the connotations of the term, or stop calling computers "machines".'

The alternative presumably is to call computers a 'species' and thereby insidiously strengthen the comparison between them and people. If the machine is admitted to the realm of nature then its evolution to a position superior to man will seem so much more inevitable. Of course, such an admission further downgrades the definition of man, but that is what so much artificial intelligence research and psychology seems intent on doing, incidentally redefining anything else that gets in the way. A serious international computer conference recently ended by recommending that languages, such as English, should be redesigned to become better adapted to computer needs. 'What is needed . . . is agreement on closely spaced and carefully defined meanings, so that existing language can begin to achieve the precision of definition needed for the new computing.' No one seems to have realized, and certainly no one has protested at, the implications of such a statement, to alter human culture to suit the convenience of an electronic tool!

Since Alan Turing's original thoughts about artificial intelligence, the notion of machines that evolve has continued. The evolutionary theme has two strands to it. First, by referring to developments as evolutionary, the idea arises that machines evolve into more powerful machines, first of all aided by man's own ingenuity, but later by the capabilities of the machines themselves. Turing expressed this idea in terms of building different forms of 'child-machine' until one was 'selected' that was more fit for survival. Today the 'evolution' of super computers is discussed more in terms of new generation machines 'assisting' in the design of superior ones, until the leap-frogging of machine intelligence evolves into a higher realm than human thought.

The second evolutionary theme concerns the evolution of man. The line of thought goes something like this: man evolved over millions of years and has a certain intelligence. Man himself is reaching the capacity to develop (or evolve) machines that will be superior to humans. This is part of a continuing line of evolution. Hence one scientist wrote: 'It is possible to look on Man himself as a product of an evolutionary process of developing robots, begotten by simpler robots, back to the primordial slime'. Man, here, is redefined as nothing but a robot, in a mindless chain of evolving robots, whose only purpose is to assist in the evolution of yet higher robots.

The incapacity of man to solve his problems is then blamed on his limited intelligence. 'It is certainly the best that evolution has been able to achieve in the time that it has had at its disposal', writes Christopher Evans, continuing, 'there is no reason to suppose that, given ... time and evolutionary pressure, further advances in human intelligence might not result. Unfortunately the world is in such a perilous condition that we do not have the time to hang around for this to happen' (p. 195). So he suggests that man play God and speed up the evolutionary pace in order to develop machines that will be people's intellectual superiors.

The interesting thing about artificial intelligence is that it is an area of technological development where many of the aims and motivations behind the research are quite explicitly stated. The development of machines, another species of information-processing creature, to supersede man is being actively advocated. Dr Robert Jastrow, head of the Godard Space Flight Centre and a prominent and senior scientist in the United States, has announced a programme to alter the course of biological evolution so that the human species becomes replaced by 'silicon-based intelligence'. As Weizenbaum has commented, this is a programme for genocide.

The explicit aim of producing the Ultra-Intelligent Machine is found frequently in statements by the leaders of computing science. H. A. Simon took up the challenge when he wrote, 'Not just on behalf of myself, but on behalf of the entire group of people working in the field, I accept the obligation [to get a machine to learn language and attain higher intelligence] and hope that one of us will produce the requisite program before long'.

Specific parts of human culture are also being attacked until they submit to 'understanding'. Professor Marvin Minsky, of Massachusetts Institute of Technology, has said that we will understand the creative processes of musical composition, when computers have been programmed to write good music. Research on the computer understanding of music is currently being conducted. Donald Michie, commenting on the desirability of machine 'understanding' of creative, human processes, suggests that this method of extending human culture is a way for man to gain immortality. H. A. Simon has gone so far as to comment that the human species could acceptably be superseded by intelligent machines because we would have 'cultural descendants'. There would be an immortality of human culture carried on by our electronic successors. Michie says of such developments that they cannot be classified as 'anything but good'. These are not the exotic writings of science fiction writers, but the considered opinions and thoughts of the leading scientists in artificial intelligence research.

The super computer is envisaged as a machine that will rapidly replace all human functions, and will be able to provide all human needs; but where does that leave people? Some suggestions have been made that we shall become the pets and playthings of the machine whose ancestors are the pets and playthings of us here and now. A more sinister speculation can be presented whereby the logical outcome of replacing human functions is simply to dispense with humans altogether. The rapid development of the technology, hand in hand with its military application, could be argued as evidence in favour of such a scenario. If the point of microtechnology is, at least partially, to maximize the profits of the corporations who promote it, then maybe the elimination of 'useless' sections of the population would be the logically economic path to pursue. Such a course also seems compatible with the 'men as pets' idea, because the computer world will not want too many domestic animals.

Another path towards higher machine intelligence that is being pursued is through man–machine symbiosis. The notion of a person being 'plugged in' to a computer to augment the brain seems ridiculous and far fetched. However, at least two experiments have already been successfully completed in attempts to achieve this merger of man and machine. In one experiment aircraft pilots were trained in a bio-feedback technique to control their brain patterns on an electro-encephalogram machine. By thinking of particular phrases they could alter their EEG patterns sufficiently for a computer to spot the difference. Such thoughts were then used as information requests, so that when a pilot thought 'airspeed' his EEG pattern altered and was interpreted by the computer; it could then give the pilot the requested information. As modern pilots, especially fighter pilots, need information very rapidly and, because of the speeds at which they are moving, cannot afford to lower their eyes to look at their instrument panel, such a device has great potential. If the pilot thinks 'altitude' and instantly the aircraft's altitude is flashed up on to the windshield, through which he is looking (the information focused at infinity, so the pilot does not have to adjust his eye), then this rather crude man–machine interaction increases the effectiveness of the pilot's task.

Another man–machine symbiosis experiment, and one which has had practical application, involves pain. In this experiment a patient with severe pain in the lower half of the body has been literally plugged in to a computer. An electrode has been placed in the patient's back to contact the nerve path through the spinal column. The impulse that is transmitted to the brain and which then registers pain, has been identified; the computer, linked to the electrode, can pick up the signal before the brain does and either modify it or remove it from further transmission to the brain. In this way the computer, linked into the human central nervous system, actually controls, in a limited way, the signals reaching a person's brain, and, in this case, controls a patient's pain for him. Other experiments are being conducted that involve more direct links between the brains of animals, including monkeys, and computers.

Donald Michie writes: 'The symbiotic concept points towards our becoming not a superseded species but an augmented one'. It is a path he hopes research will take, but he warns that such symbiotic systems will need to have protective devices built into them, in case the machine element of the partnership finds it can dispense with the man part. He concludes: 'It will certainly be unwise for our species to apply the historical pattern of encouraging the extinction of less viable groups. In a future in which the planet is shared with intelligent machines, perpetuation of the principle could become two-edged' (p. 133).

Man–machine symbiosis brings together the two areas of modern research interest: life and mind. Another expression of the combination of these qualities could be found in the idea of augmenting animal life by suitable genetic manipulation and the combination of computing intelligence implanted in the body of the beast. Such an enterprise can then open up the prospect of designing species via genetic engineering giving the modern scientist and technologist scope for almost unlimited tampering with nature, stimulating so-called evolutionary processes, for playing God. Although science can tell us nothing about what 'life' is, it is assumed that we can hand it on to our machine successors. The aim of computer science is 'to populate the world with a new machine species', as Professor Frank George has written, adding, 'and that, I believe, is exactly what we are going to do'.

How far along that road we have travelled is difficult to evaluate. The ideas being propagated are mostly fantastic projections and the common small computer seems an innocent enough machine. The Hacker syndrome, which is effectively hypnosis induced by the computer, combined with known cases of what amounts to extra-sensory perception, of mind influencing machine, suggests that computer circuits have a potential for connection with consciousness that is even exploited in the cheapest calculator. That potential seems to have been unconsciously grasped by people working in computer research and is manifest in their often far-fetched ideas. The small computer can stimulate that potential and when connected to a network can amplify it. Plugging in the machine connects us to a world where human characteristics are redefined in terms of the electronic device and where we find none of man's highest emotion, love.

11 THE SILICON IDOL

Professor Joseph Weizenbaum has said, 'I'm coming close to believing that the computer is inherently anti-human—an invention of the devil'. He speaks from a long, close professional involvement with computers and artificial intelligence research at one of the most prestigious academic establishments in the world, MIT. That is one of many impassioned things he has said about the impact of computers on society and on people and raises the question why such an apparently extreme statement should be uttered. A simple answer can be given in this form.

Putting faith in false idols has always dehumanized people, led people into blind alleys. Idols made by 'the work of human hands' are inevitably false idols, and, being idols, reflect their incomplete, inhuman, qualities back on to those who believe in them. The mirror image is less real than the real object. Man, redefined by a man-made idol, must always be diminished. In the last few years we have built idols of silicon, and our increasing belief in them makes us all more inhuman, for the silicon idol is *not* human. In so far as it is a parody of a human, a perversion of the real thing, it can be described as devilish, not good, not of God. The computer, seen as the current pinnacle of technological development, is inherently anti-human because it redefines man at such a lowly level and with such power. Its powerful effect, its capacity to take over, to act as a general palliative to being human, which seems so comforting that we accept its consequences unquestioningly, is what makes people believe in it, gains itself its worshippers. Yet it is a technology that springs from motives of power from a military/industrial base with intentions to pervert truth, and to subjugate the population. Like other technologies that have the same parentage, we allow its progress until it seems too late to do anything about it, and then we find ways to adapt ourselves to it.

This last point encapsulates the difficulties inherent in the relationship between technology and social control. New techniques are brought into the social arena by their developers and financial entrepreneurs and then people have to adapt to them. The process is undemocratic and yet it seems quite ridiculous to contemplate the idea of voting against a technology. Besides which the question never arises. Political parties, from the extreme left to the far right, are concerned not with the technological means of production but how the wealth generated is allocated and controlled. There is almost no political debate about more fundamental underlying issues concerning the nature of society, except in pressure groups concerned with ecology, feminism, and peace. In mainstream politics choice is limited to different versions of the same technological society. Such choices as are offered are presented as 'freedoms', just as the new technology is presented as conferring freedoms on people. What the new technology can do is to provide mass-produced goods in a wider variety (almost unlimited variety actually) of styles than could the mechanical production line. It can provide dozens of television and information channels rather than the few we now have; but this does *not* give us freedom, it merely gives us more of the same, with less real choice because not only are there no real alternatives offered, but the flood of similar things is overwhelming and numbing. The freedom we are offered is the freedom to become intoxicated by technological narcotics.

Until political and social commentators come to recognize the importance of technology in defining social and political structures then ironical situations will remain such as the following. Unemployment levels in the Western countries are high and rising. In Britain they are running at a level considered only a few years ago as quite unacceptable. Part of the reason for such high unemployment has been the world recession, inflation, high oil prices and the changing pattern of world trade. Another part is the new microelectronic technology, although I believe this still to be a minor contributor. Whilst governments talk about their desire to reduce unemployment they are at the same time offering larger incentives to firms to automate than to take on extra staff. Alongside this, the move towards cable television and the widespread introduction of information channels into homes looks like a palliative to unemployment. The way society is shaping it seems as if it is being deliberately engineered to have few jobs and a large amount of 'entertainment'. The new technology thereby acts as a powerful weapon in maintaining social structures, tightening control over the population and selling the deal as both inevitable and progressive. It is, after all, the continuation of the progress made over the last three hundred years.

The promise of flexibility and freedom offered by computing technology is an illusion; just as it is an illusion to say that flexible (that is computer/robot controlled) production gives a wider choice of consumer goods, when the real choice should be between consumer goods and other options. The new technology and computing techniques are not more humanistic, as the psychologists claim, simply because they are not mechanistic. They are mechanistic in the sense that they stem from the same source, the same philosophy, the same motivation as the other techniques. Their flexibility, the softness of computer technologies, is merely a disguise.

The soft technology offers the potential to monitor every person, every vehicle, every home and work place by civil and military authorities and to hand over to them the possibility of detailed control of people's lives.

The method of selling computer technology is useful to look at, because the propaganda illustrates several things I have discussed. Information systems are being pushed by stressing their low cost. For example, one advertisement says:

In the future, shopping could be easier and more convenient. We could simply telephone the shop, view the goods on our television, then order what we want via a keypad and make payment through a credit card attachment on our set. Information technology, therefore, would give to us all a sort of service that in the past we just would not have been able to afford.

Are people asking for such a service? Do people no longer want any social interaction with other human beings? How do you examine goods via television, unless all goods become so uniform and packaged that it no longer matters? Will the technology give this service to *all* or just to those who *can* afford it? Do we want to afford it? These are just a few questions such a passage brings to my mind. When the advertising is scrutinized by such questions it becomes clear how irrelevant the new technology is in response to the real needs of people. Other propaganda sells the notion that computer technology 'looks after us', taking on a role of super-parent, a caring, benign technology that can do for us what we are incapable of doing for ourselves. It is even claimed that the new technology provides us with a 'better understanding of how to care for people', when, in fact, the reality of the situation is that it displaces people from positions of helping others, interferes between people really relating to each other, prevents people from taking responsibility.

'The important thing to remember about the Information Technology (IT) revolution, is that its effects are friendly. And ... like most revolutions, IT is irresistible.' So reads government propaganda for the technology that allows unlimited power to monitor people's lives and that enables weapons of great devastation to pinpoint their targets more precisely. The information about information technology that is disseminated widely by press, television, radio, science magazines, schools and universities is all based on the same assumptions and the same myths. Belief in the Silicon Idol is already widespread and the world is being redefined by the impact of the computer.

The metaphor of the computer, the machine that 'thinks', redefines the world in terms of 'information'. People are seen as 'information-processing systems', the universe is interpreted as a vast 'information system'; all human and social interactions are analysed or discussed or even just referred to in terms of information content. Money becomes information. Language, which contains such richness of meaning, words being symbols of whole hierarchies of meaning, is redefined in terms of pure information. Books are now being produced that contain striped lines instead of words, so that a 'light pen', connected to a speaking computer, can 'read' the book to a child. Our imaginations, then, are seen as simply information.

Personal relations are being reinterpreted in terms of information transfer. Seymour Papert urges that children should gain 'self-confidence through their relationship with the machine', but presumably at the expense of their ability to relate to other people. Policies are now strongly directed to capturing children as young as possible to adapt their upbringing and education to the needs of computers and their controllers. The brave new world being planned will have such people in it as have adapted to the ways of the machine.

The movement towards the quantification of the world seeks to reduce all complex meaning, subtlety and quality to pure information, which can then be coded in binary notation. Culture is degraded, redefined in terms of the crudities of computer graphics, whatever can be put on a television screen, denuded of quality. Consider the comparison between text on a television set and the reading of a good book. Even the feel of the paper adds a dimension of quality to the one, a quality totally missing in the other. A computer-readable alphabet is of appalling design, containing no aesthetic quality at all. We are being acclimatized to an artificial environment that is just plain ugly.

Religion is degraded in a computer world into being at best a way to find a pathway for individual development, guided by suitable software. Machines for answering prayers are as obscene a notion as robot lovers outskilling human partners in the art of seduction or the handing over of children to be educated by an expert systems teacher. Any concept which entails that people can enhance their humanity from the example of a synthetic machine is morally ugly.

Products are degraded in the same way. The object made by a machine, however 'individual', just lacks that quality of a craft-produced, humanly endowed object. Unless there is an appreciable swing back towards a craft economy, more and more people will have their lives and environments filled with dehumanized objects and the effect on them will be to numb them further. People's expectations are also redefined by the machine. Even simple addition is handed over to a calculator rather than done 'in the head'. 'How did people work out such things in the past?' we ask ourselves, forgetting that people managed more than adequately. We have been redefined by the computer as inadequate.

Christopher Evans, in *The Mighty Micro* says, 'Even the most optimistic of human beings will admit that our world is in a most dangerously muddled state, and Man, unaided, is unlikely to be able to do much to improve it' (p. 197). This plea for 'alien intelligences' to come to help us is a sign of how inadequate we appear to have become. Evans, in common with most commentators, does not turn around to see why we are out of our depth, but pins his hopes on our being saved by a Silicon Idol.

Already there are signs that we, human beings, have given up. Marvin Minsky of MIT wrote:

The argument, based on the fact that reliable computers do only that which they are instructed to do, has a basic flaw; it does not follow that the programmer has full knowledge (and therefore full responsibility and credit) of what will ensue. For certainly the programmer may set up an evolutionary system whose limitations are to him unclear and possibly incomprehensible. (p. 12)

If the programmer is not responsible, is it surprising that the head of a computing laboratory can write, '. . . the computer has been incorporating itself . . . into most functions that are fundamental to the support, protection and development of our society'? With the added reminder that '. . . there is no stemming this trend in computer development'. Responsibility for what we do, as individuals, is no longer deemed necessary. The machine has taken over. It will care for us.

In the developed countries people have been separating themselves from nature and from one another as human beings until they no longer feel able to cope. We need our dependency-creating technologies because we have become dependent on them. The propaganda mentions a range of domestic products—freezers, toasters, dishwashers—and comments, 'of course it would be possible to live without these things, but it wouldn't be very easy or pleasant'. I have no freezer, toaster or dishwasher and yet I lead a pleasant and really very easy life. But is life meant to be 'easy and pleasant'? Is that all the human condition is about? Should not life be rich in experience, meaningful and sometimes painful? Is it a prime obligation for us to remove all pain from the world? If nature evolved pain then maybe pain has its functions, and is not just a thing to be eradicated. Besides, our painkillers—toasters, television, computers—do not really remove pain, but shift our attention to something else. Pain is what happens to other people, something we should experience only at second hand, via information technology. We no longer recognize spiritual pain, the distressed soul, although we suffer from that disease more than any other. Turing's own suicide was a symptom of that, and the degree of depression, loneliness, despair and frustration in evidence in 'advanced' societies indicates a malaise of the spirit that we seek to cure by increasing the poison that causes it.

When we look at 'primitive' societies and at the things those people recognize, we find that the beliefs, rituals, myths and true gods they worship are dismissed as 'superstitions'; we try to cure them of their unscientific, old-fashioned, illiberal and crude ways by offering them the very thing that denies us what they have. We try to substitute our false idol for their real ones, believing our parody of truth is superior to their vision.

It is the poor, undeveloped and 'primitive' peoples of this world that in some ways will suffer more from information technology's imperialism and in some ways will suffer less. The poor countries certainly suffer now, because the West has offered them the rich life, the materialistic life that has been obtained at their expense. They can never hope to attain standards of living such as those of Europe and the USA. Computer technology will widen the gap between rich and poor, nations and individuals. The false hopes and promises offered should be withdrawn. The under-developed should be allowed to make their own choices, and not have our choices, our technologies imposed on them. They will suffer less than we do by finding their own way, solving their own problems, taking responsibility for themselves, maintaining a more spiritual orientation on life. By rejecting a technology and a way of life alien to their traditions they will gain much more than they can ever hope to achieve by following the West down a path that turns rapidly into a slippery slope. If that is true of unwesternized nations, of the poor people of the world, then it is also true of the poor people in our own society: and not just the poor.

Computer technology is not just flexible, it is also clean. Microtechnology consumes little power and uses up scarcely any raw materials (although the innumerable products the robot factories are supposed to produce will consume vast quantities), nor does it cause pollution. Such are the claims. And yet, as in all discussion of the subject, the subject matter of the discussion is confined to the physical, quantifiable levels of reality. There is never any mention, with respect to microtechnology, of the spiritual effects of surrounding ourselves by an electronic web of artificiality. The absence of physical pollution is counteracted by a non-material pollution, a pollution of the mind and spirit. Physical manifestations of that malaise will inevitably appear.

When Professor Newell spoke of 'enchantment' he was redefining the word. He was referring to an enchantment by which, through the power of our technology, the world is made to appear animated and magical. The world was disenchanted by the same processes that have given rise to the technology that parodies that lost enchantment. The rise of modern technology changed man's perception of a world whose hierarchies of spiritual, psychic and material values, were understood, at least in part. The power of scientific thought enabled the material world to be manipulated more effectively than the magician had done in the psychic world. In the seventeenth century, science defeated magic in the quest for manipulative power over the world. The enchantment Newell describes is modern magic, a magic of the material rather than psychic world, but one that is just as dangerous, just as spiritually damaging. The Luddites were a minority group of witch hunters in a world where material witchcraft, engineered through science, had taken hold. Information technology does re-enchant the world. It is modern magic, as Weizenbaum suggests, and the invention of the devil.

Evil works in this world by mimicking good. The devil tells nine truths to sell one lie. A technology developed as an instrument of human destruction, that dehumanizes lives, is shown to be benign. Criminals are caught, babies' lives are saved, diseases are diagnosed early; these things bestow apparent benefits. Their cost is high. Technology is not neutral, it is capable of being used or abused, employed for good or evil purposes. Weizenbaum, again, has commented that it seems a universal law that anything that can be abused, will be abused. But this technology was born destructive. The euphoria it engenders is like a magic spell. It enchants people into false belief in a false god.

How, then, can we face this creation? What can people do about the 'inevitable' intrusion of computer technology into every nook and cranny of the world? Is there a sane response? I think there is, but it can only spring from individual people coming to understand the situation they are faced with. A sane response to the technology must surely begin with a recognition that the new technology is harmful, is irrelevant, comes from the desire to control and dominate, and is best left alone, not compromised with. There is a story that comes from an ancient Chinese sage which was quoted by Werner Heizenberg in his book *The Physicist's Conception of Nature*. I quote it here for its contemporary relevance.

As Tzu-Gung was travelling through the regions north of the river Han, he saw an old man working in his vegetable garden. He had dug an irrigation ditch. The man would descend into a well, fetch up a vessel of water in his arms and pour it into the ditch. While his efforts were tremendous the results appeared to be very meagre. Tzu-Gung said, 'There is a way whereby you can irrigate a hundred ditches in one day, and whereby you can do much with little effort. Would you not like to hear of it?'

Then the gardener stood up, looked at him and said, 'And what would that be?' Tzu-Gung replied. 'You take a wooden lever, weighted at the back and light in front. In this way you can bring up water so quickly that it just gushes out. This is called a draw-well.'

Then anger rose up in the old man's face, and he said, 'I have heard my teacher say that whoever uses machines does his work like a machine. He who does his work like a machine grows the heart of a machine, and he who carries the heart of a machine in his breast loses his simplicity. He who has lost his simplicity becomes unsure in the strivings of his soul. Uncertainty in the strivings of the soul is something which does not agree with honest sense. It is not that I do not know of such things; I am ashamed to use them.'

Confronted by a complex technology, our desire to know what to do, what honest sense is, can only come from the values we regard as the highest motives of our humanity. In order to develop a course of action we need to think out our real needs, and then to try to discriminate between what helps and what hinders attaining those needs. Different people will express themselves in very different ways, some maybe becoming twentieth-century Luddites, others maybe just refusing to participate in an artificial world of electronic madness. We need to wean ourselves from the dependency the technology creates and that is often painful. From my home the television has gone and the pocket calculator is banished. The telephone still seems an unwanted necessity. The act of discrimination is not easy, but life does become more meaningful and more human.

Our world has lost its simplicity and has become unsure in the striving of its soul. Putting faith in a Silicon Idol enmeshes us further in the dense image of the world and does not agree with honest sense. We need to be informed about the machines that 'think' but we should become ashamed to use them. In the face of a threatening technology we should attempt to seek wisdom. In the face of a world of increasing automation we should remember our humanity and what it springs from and use our honest sense for the benefit and use of life and love.

FURTHER READING

Chapter 1

Barrett, W., *The Illusion of Technique* (Kimber, London, 1978).
Evans, C., *The Mighty Micro* (Gollancz, London, 1979).
Frude, N., *The Intimate Machine* (Century, London, 1983).
Hofstader, D. R., *Gödel, Escher, Bach* (Basic Books, New York, 1979).
McLuhan, M., *Understanding Media* (R. K. P., London, 1964).
Schumacher, E. F., *A Guide for the Perplexed* (Cape, London, 1977).
Turing, A. M., 'Computing Machinery and Intelligence', *Mind*, LIX, no. 236 (1950), p. 433.
Weizenbaum, J., *Computer Power and Human Reason* (Freeman, San Francisco, 1976).

Chapter 2

Cooper, M. J., *What Computers can do* (Maclaren, London, 1969).
Hartley, M. G. and Healey, M., *A First Course in Computer Technology* (McGraw Hill, London, 1978).
Holingdale, S. H. and Toothill, G. C., *Electronic Computers* (Penguin, Harmondsworth, 1965).
Hunt, R. and Shelley, J., *Computers and Commonsense* (Prentice Hall, London, 1979).
Lippiatt, A. G., *The Architecture of Small Computer Systems* (Prentice Hall, London, 1979).

Chapter 3

Debenham, M. J., *Microprocessors* (Pergamon, Oxford, 1979).
Marsh, P., *The Silicon Chip Book* (Abacus, London, 1981).
Renmore, C. D., *The Silicon Chip and You* (Sheldon, London, 1979).
Scientific American, *Microelectronics* (Freeman, San Francisco, 1977).
Simons, G. L., *Introducing Microprocessors* (N.C.C., London, 1979).

Chapter 4

Forester, T. (ed.), *The Microelectronics Revolution* (Blackwell, Oxford, 1980).
Large, P., *The Micro Revolution* (Fontana, London, 1980).
Weizenbaum, J., 'Technological Intoxication', in *Faith and Science in an Unjust World*, R. L. Shinn (ed.) (W.C.C., Geneva, 1980).
Zorkoczy, P., *Information Technology* (Pitman, London, 1982).

Chapter 5

Barron, I. and Curnow, R., *The Future with Microelectronics* (Open University Press, Milton Keynes, 1979).
Bell, D., *The Coming of Post-Industrial Society* (Basic Books, New York, 1973).
George, F. H. and Humphries, J. D. (eds.), *The Robots are Coming* (N.C.C., London, 1974).
Jones, T. (ed.), *Microelectronics and Society* (Open University Press, Milton Keynes, 1980).
Martin, J., *The Wired Society* (Prentice Hall, New Jersey, 1978).
Raphael, B., *The Thinking Computer* (Freeman, San Francisco, 1976).

Chapter 6

Acquaviva, S. S., *The Decline of the Sacred in Industrial Society* (Blackwell, Oxford, 1979).
Berman, M., *The Re-enchantment of the World* (Cornell University Press, Ithaca, 1981).
Biram, J., *Teknosis* (Arlington, London, 1978).
Black, M., 'Is Scientific Neutrality a Myth?', in *Are Science and Technology Neutral?*, J. Lipscombe and B. Williams (eds.) (SISCON, Butterworths, London, 1979).
Derry, T. K. and Williams, T. I., *The Short History of Technology* (Oxford University Press, Oxford, 1960).
Dickson, D., *Alternative Technology* (Fontana, London, 1974).
Ellul, J., *The Technological Society* (Knopf, New York, 1964).
Hooykas, R., *Religion and the Rise of Modern Science* (Scottish Academic Press, Edinburgh, 1972).
Landes, D., *The Unbound Prometheus* (Cambridge University Press, New York, 1969).
McLuhan, M., *Understanding Media* (R.K.P., London, 1964).
Mumford, L., *Technics and Civilization* (R.K.P., London, 1934).
Northbourne, Lord, *Religion and the Modern World* (Dent, London, 1963).

Richardson, W. J., *Heidegger* (Nijhoff, The Hague, 1967).
Rose, H. and Rose, S., *Science and Society* (Penguin, Harmondsworth, 1969).
Shallis, M. J., *On Time* (Burnett Books, London, 1982).
Simondon, G., *Du mode d'existence des objets techniques* (Aubier, Paris, 1958).
Thomas, K., *Religion and the Decline of Magic* (Weidenfeld and Nicolson, London, 1971).

Chapter 7

Atkins, P., *The Creation* (Freeman, London, 1981).
Boden, M. A., *Artificial Intelligence and Natural Man* (Harvester, Brighton, 1977).
Bohm, D., *Wholeness and the Implicate Order* (R.K.P., London, 1980).
Evans, C., *The Making of the Micro* (Gollancz, London, 1981).
Guénon, R., *The Reign of Quantity* (Penguin, New York, 1972).
Hodges, A., *Alan Turing: the Enigma* (Burnett Books, London, 1983).
Hyman, A., *Charles Babbage* (Oxford University Press, Oxford, 1982).
Kidder, T., *The Soul of a New Machine* (Allan Lane, London, 1982).
Marsh, P., 'The Mechanization of Man', *New Scientist*, 89, no. 1240 (1981), p. 418.
Schumacher, E. F., *A Guide for the Perplexed* (Cape, London, 1977).
Turing, A., from *Mind*—see Chapter 1.

Chapter 8

Barron, I. and Curnow, R., *The Future with Microelectronics* (Open University Press, Milton Keynes, 1979).
Bell, D., *The Coming of Post-Industrial Society* (Basic Books, New York, 1973).
Bell, D., 'The Social Framework of the Information Society', in Forester—see Chapter 4.
Jones, T. (ed.), *Microelectronics and Society* (Open University Press, Milton Keynes, 1980).
Laver, M., *Computers and Social Change* (Cambridge University Press, Cambridge, 1980).
Mander, G., *Four Arguments for the Elimination of Television* (Harvester Press, Brighton, 1980).
Rada, J., *The Impact of Micro-electronics* (I.L.O., Geneva, 1980).
Schumacher, E. F., *Good Work* (Cape, London, 1979).
Stonier, T., 'The Impact of Microprocessors on Employment', in Forester—see Chapter 4.

Chapter 9

Albury, D. and Schwartz, J., *Partial Progress* (Pluto, London, 1982).

Burnham, D., *The Rise of the Computer State* (Weidenfeld and Nicolson, London, 1983).

Clarke, A. C., *2001* (Hutchinson, London, 1968).

Lowi, T. J., 'The Political Aspect of Information Technology', in Forester—see Chapter 4.

Talbot, J. R., *The Management Guide to Computer Security* (Gower, Farnborough, 1981).

Weizenbaum, J., 'Where are we going?', in Forester—see Chapter 4.

Chapter 10

Asimov, I., *I Robot* (Panther, London, 1968).

Barr, A. and Feigenbaum, E. A. (eds.), *Handbook of Artificial Intelligence* (Pitman, London, 1981).

Boden, M. A., *Artificial Intelligence and Natural Man* (Harvester, Brighton, 1977).

Colby, K. M., 'Computer Simulation of a Neurotic Process', in *Computer Simulation of Personality*, S. Tomkins and S. Messick (eds.) (Wiley, New York, 1963).

Colby, K. M., Gilbert, J. P. and Watt, J. B., 'A Computer Method of Psychotherapy', *Journal of Nervous and Mental Disease*, 142, no. 2 (1966), p. 148.

Evans, C., *The Mighty Micro* (Gollancz, London, 1979).

George, F. H., *Man the Machine* (Paladin, London, 1979).

Jastrow, R., *The Enchanted Loom—mind in the Universe* (Simon and Schuster, New York, 1982).

Michie, D., *On Machine Intelligence* (Edinburgh University Press, Edinburgh, 1974).

Michie, D., 'The Social Aspects of Artificial Intelligence', in Jones (ed.)—see Chapter 5.

Miller, G. A., 'Language, Learning and Models of the Mind' (unpublished MS quoted in Weizenbaum, *Computer Power and Human Reason*, 1976).

Minsky, M., *Semantic Information Processing* (MIT Press, Cambridge, 1968).

Newell, A., *Fairy Tales*, Viewpoints No. 3 (Carnegie-Mellon University, Pittsburgh, 1976).

Raphael, B., *The Thinking Computer* (Freeman, San Francisco, 1976).

Simon, H. A., *The Sciences of the Artificial* (MIT Press, Cambridge, 1969).

Simon, H. A., 'What Computers Mean for Man and Society', in Forester—see Chapter 4.

Simon, H. A. and Newell, A., 'Heuristic Problem Solving', *Operations Research*, vol. 6 (1958), p. 8.

Weizenbaum, J., *Computer Power and Human Reason* (Freeman, San Francisco, 1976).

Weizenbaum, J., 'Technological Intoxification'—see Chapter 4.

Winograd, T., *Understanding Natural Language* (New York Academic Press, New York, 1972).

Zemenek, H., 'The Human Being and the Automaton', in *Human Choice and Computers*, E. Mumford and H. Sackman (eds.) (North-Holland, Amsterdam, 1975).

INDEX